# The Kids' Fun-Filled Question & Answer Book

Text by
Jane Parker Resnick

Illustrated by
Anthony Tallarico

Incorporated

Copyright © 1998 Kidsbooks, Inc. and Anthony Tallarico
3535 West Peterson Avenue
Chicago, IL 60659

Manufactured in the United States of America

# Why do dolphins seem smart?

They're brainy. A dolphin's brain, in relation to its body size, is as big as a human's. But a dolphin's brain is much simpler than the human brain. Dolphins are naturally curious and playful. They learn quickly and even understand some language. Because this behavior seems "human," we think they're smart. And, in their way, they are.

## WHAT'S THE SMELLIEST THING IN THE WORLD?

There are thousands of smells in the world and millions of opinions on what is the worst. The cause of a nasty smell is its chemical combination. For example, rotten eggs could be one of the smelliest things in the world. The odor is from *sulfur dioxide*. And if you ever come across the chemical *ethyl mercaptan* you won't forget it. It is said to smell like a combination of rotting cabbage, garlic, onions, burned toast, and sewer gas.

## HOW DO WAVES FORM IN THE OCEAN?

Waves start with wind, not water. Picture the wind moving across the surface of the ocean, lifting the water. When the wind blows harder, the waves get bigger. When the winds are calm, waves are usually no more than a few feet high. But in a storm, they may be whipped up to 60 feet tall. One of the highest waves recorded in the Pacific Ocean was 112 feet high—a wall of water taller than a 10-story building!

# WHO WAS HOUDINI?

## HOW DOES A ROCKET SOUND IN SPACE?

The greatest escape artist of all time. Harry Houdini (1874-1926) was a magician who created contraptions of ropes, handcuffs, tires, and chains from which only he could escape. He was nailed inside boxes. He was trapped in water-filled tanks. He was wrapped up in a straight-jacket and dropped in the ocean. But he always got free.

Like one hand clapping—there's no sound at all. Sound is created by "sound waves," a movement of the molecules that make up air. In space there is no air. Therefore, there are no waves and no sound.

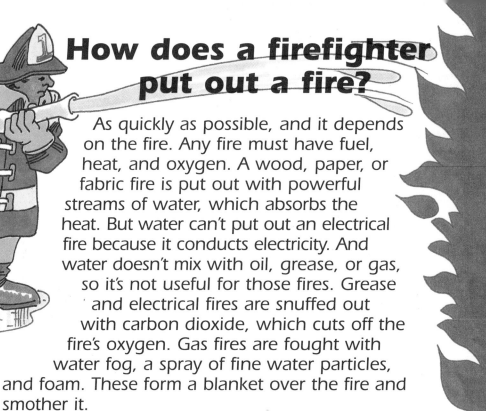

# How does a firefighter put out a fire?

As quickly as possible, and it depends on the fire. Any fire must have fuel, heat, and oxygen. A wood, paper, or fabric fire is put out with powerful streams of water, which absorbs the heat. But water can't put out an electrical fire because it conducts electricity. And water doesn't mix with oil, grease, or gas, so it's not useful for those fires. Grease and electrical fires are snuffed out with carbon dioxide, which cuts off the fire's oxygen. Gas fires are fought with water fog, a spray of fine water particles, and foam. These form a blanket over the fire and smother it.

## What causes chicken pox?

You usually catch it from a friend, because it's *contagious*. The scientific name is "varicella," and the cause is a virus. Once you've got it, there's not much to do but wait until it's over—and try not to scratch. Chicken pox is itchy. The pox are small skin eruptions that make your skin look a little like a chicken's.

CAN I GET PEOPLE POX?

I'D RATHER HAVE PIZZA!!

# WHO WERE THE GLADIATORS?

The Roman Empire was a great civilization with a cruel form of entertainment—the fighting of gladiators. These men were prisoners of war, slaves, or criminals. They were forced to fight each other in a great stadium while the Romans cheered. Most of the time, the gladiators battled until one gruesomely killed the other. These fights were usually part of festivals that sometimes went on for months. All this "fun" lasted from 264 B.C. to A.D. 404.

## WHAT MAKES A DIAMOND SPARKLE?

You can't have sparkle without light, and diamonds make the most of it. A diamond is a pure carbon crystal formed beneath the earth under severe heat and pressure. But it doesn't sparkle in its natural form. Diamond cutters cut *facets*—small surfaces—into the stone that catch the light. A cut diamond has the ability to bend the light and reflect it more than any other substance, and that makes it sparkle.

# Have aliens ever visited Earth?

Scientists have no evidence that extraterrestrial beings have ever been on our planet. But that doesn't stop some people from believing that aliens have dropped by now and then. There have been many claims of UFO sightings around the world, and a few folks even claim to have been abducted by aliens!

Dear Mom,
Having a wonderful time on earth – wish you were here!
Love,
GORZAT II

MOM,
MARS 10013

The idea is so fascinating to real believers that they don't need scientific proof to think it's true.

THIS IS NOT MY LUCKY DAY!!

# What are spittlebugs?

Not too many bugs are a pretty sight, but spittle-bugs are stuck with an ugly name. "Spittle" is a word for the bubbly saliva mess we all think of as "spit." Spittlebugs are small jumping insects, less than half an inch long, that look like tiny frogs. In their *nymph*, or infant stage, they live in a frothy, spittlelike mass, which they create themselves. So "spittlebug," after all, is a name they deserve.

# WHY DO WE GET GOOSEBUMPS?

When we get cold, the hairs on our body stand up straight. When this happens, our skin pushes up into little bumps. Our body may be trying to keep us warm, but the hairs we have just don't do the trick! If we had fur or feathers that stood on end, the air between them would hold in the heat and keep the cold out. So, unfortunately, we remain cold and simply look like geese whose feathers have just been plucked.

# WHO INVENTED ICE CREAM?

It remains a mystery. Most historians agree that Italy's Catherine de Medici, with help from chef Bernardo Buontalenti, introduced "cream ice" to France in 1533. The cold, creamy confection wasn't known as "ice cream" until it reached America in the 1700s, where it became wildly popular. First president George Washington spent a great deal of money on the expensive dessert. He even liked to make it at home with a "Cream Machine for Making Ice." The price dropped a century later when Jacob Fussell, a Baltimore dairyman, invented the first ice-cream factory.

# WHY IS

## CONSIDERED AN UNLUCKY NUMBER?

Poor number 13. People have been uneasy about it since primitive man counted his ten fingers and two feet and came up with 12. After that came the unknown—13. And anything unknown is scary. As with all superstitions, there is no reasonable answer. But that doesn't mean people don't take it seriously. Many hotels and office buildings don't have a 13th floor!

## What happens to bears when they hibernate?

Not much. When most animals hibernate, their body temperature drops and their breathing slows down. Not bears. They just sleep away most of the winter in a normal, but very drowsy, state. Cubs are born in the winter, and the mothers practically sleep through the whole ordeal! Everyone may get up and walk around for awhile, but then it's back to the den to sleep until spring.

DO NOT DISTURB

Z-Z-Z-Z-

7

# Has anyone ever found pirate's treasure?

Yes! More than 100,000 objects were recovered from the *Whydah*, a ship captured in 1717 by the pirate Samuel Bellamy off the coast of the Bahamas. The shipwrecked vessel was *salvaged*, or brought up from the sea, in 1984. Among the treasures was a collection of gold jewelry, created by the Akan people of Africa.

## WHAT IS AIR MADE OF?

It feels like nothing, but air is definitely something. It's invisible, but it's not weightless. Air is made up of gases, mostly nitrogen and some oxygen with a small amount of argon. There's also a bit of water vapor. A hundred miles of air rises above your head—or sits on your shoulders.

## DOES A CAT REALLY HAVE NINE LIVES?

It just seems that way. Cats are fast and flexible—and they have an excellent sense of balance. They bound out of the way of danger. They fall from scary heights and land on their feet. They squeeze out of tight spots. Cats escape harm so often that people say they have "nine lives."

# WHY DO FLIES HAVE SUCH BIG EYES?

"The better to see you with, my dear." Most insects have large eyes made up of many lenses. These are called *compound eyes*. (Some dragonflies have 300,000 lenses in each eye!) In fact, flies don't see too clearly because each lens is fixed and can't be adjusted for distance. But flies with eyes that cover most of their heads have 360-degree vision. They can see anything coming at them from any-where—which is why it's so hard to catch a fly.

## What happens to the garbage I throw away?

All 1,300 pounds? That's about how much garbage each one of us throws away every year. Some solid waste goes into landfills. These are low areas where towns build mountains of garbage. The piles are packed down and covered with dirt. Very slowly, over years, tiny living organisms called microbes break down the garbage and it decays. Some solid waste is burned in huge furnaces called incinerators. Other garbage can be *recycled*. Metal objects, such as cans, are crushed, shredded, cleaned, and melted. Then the metal is recycled, or used again. Newspapers, bottles, and plastics are also recycled.

## Are all sharks dangerous?

No—but never test a shark to find out. Fewer than a hundred people worldwide are attacked by sharks each year. Twenty kinds of sharks have been known to attack people, and a few others are considered dangerous. Whale sharks are the most friendly. They can weigh more than 30,000 pounds, but they're so gentle, sometimes divers hold on to their fins and take a ride.

## HOW CAN APES LEARN SIGN LANGUAGE?

I GET TO CELEBRATE BOTH FATHER'S AND MOTHER'S DAY!

# DO MALE ANIMALS EVER GIVE BIRTH?

No, but the sea horse does a pretty good imitation. Sea horses are fish with scaly bodies and curved tails. And they're tiny—the smallest are only 2 inches and the largest are nearly a foot long. The male doesn't give birth, but he sure looks pregnant. He has a pouch just above his tail where the female places her eggs. Then she takes off and he carries the eggs around in his bulging belly for 40 to 50 days. He even takes care of the babies after they hatch.

## WHAT'S THE DIFFERENCE BETWEEN A MOTH AND A BUTTERFLY?

*Night flight...* Moths fly mostly at dark and butterflies during the day. *Antennae...* Butterflies have long, knob-tipped antennae and moths have feathery ones. *Body shape...* Butterflies are slim and moths are chunky. But if you pick up either by the wings, you may get a fine dust on your fingers. These are the scales that prove that, despite their differences, both belong to the same group of "scaly-winged" creatures, the Lepidoptera.

Apes learn sign language based on the hand signals that deaf people use. The apes watch their trainer's hands, imitate the movements, and get a reward when they get it right. Apes can even put two signs together to make a phrase like "Want food." And, using sign language, they can "talk" to each other. A famous gorilla named Koko was the first member of her species to communicate using sign language. Since 1972 she has learned more than 1,000 signs. That's an ape with a lot to say!

# What happens when a space shuttle returns to Earth's atmosphere?

It's a hot moment. When the shuttle enters Earth's atmosphere, gravity takes hold and the surrounding air causes enormous friction. Friction causes heat. In this case, the fiery temperature is more than we can imagine—3,000°F. The shuttle is protected by special tiles on its underside. They are so good at shedding heat that they can be burning hot on one side and cool enough to touch on the other.

# WHY DOES A BOOMERANG COME BACK?

It's all in your wrist and the boomerang's arms.

Boomerang arms are curved on top and flat on the bottom like airplane wings. The wind rushing over them creates "lift," and it "flies" forward. But only one arm points into the wind. The other arm points away from the wind, creating lift in the other direction. With a good snap of the wrist, a boomerang spins very quickly. This combination of spinning and opposite lift curves its flight, guiding the boomerang back to its thrower.

# What happens when the sun sets?

GOOD NIGHT!

Nothing happens to the sun. It stays in the same place while the Earth turns on its *axis* (an imaginary line from the North Pole to the South Pole). When the Earth makes one complete turn, a day has passed. Only half the planet can be facing the sun at one time. As that side turns away from the sun, we say the sun is setting. Then we are in darkness until "tomorrow," when our place on Earth turns back to the sun again.

## WHAT IS A SLOTH?

A slow-moving, furry mammal that lives in the tropical forests of Central and South America. It lives in the trees—eating, sleeping, and maneuvering upside down, clinging with sharp claws. Sloths rarely move faster than six feet a minute. If they do come down from a tree, they only hurry—well, sort of—to another tree.

# Who created the first zoo?

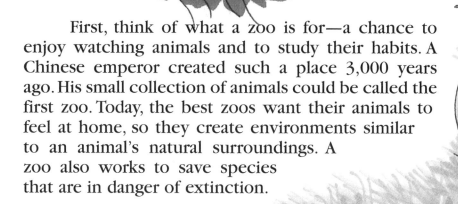

First, think of what a zoo is for—a chance to enjoy watching animals and to study their habits. A Chinese emperor created such a place 3,000 years ago. His small collection of animals could be called the first zoo. Today, the best zoos want their animals to feel at home, so they create environments similar to an animal's natural surroundings. A zoo also works to save species that are in danger of extinction.

13

# WHAT ARE THE SEVEN WONDERS

> Amazing human-made structures, most of which no longer exist.

**The Great Pyramids** at Giza, Egypt, are the only surviving ancient wonder. Tombs of pharaohs, they were built around 2600 B.C. by thousands of laborers. The Great Pyramid of Khufu is the largest, covering about 13 acres and standing 482 feet high.

**The Hanging Gardens of Babylon** were built around 600 B.C. for the queen of Babylon. The ancient city of Babylon was located close to where Baghdad, Iraq, is today. Early writings tell us that the gardens were laid out on a 300-square-foot brick terrace about 75 feet above the ground. Laborers worked around the clock to lift water from the Euphrates River to water the flowers.

**The Temple of Artemis at Ephesus** was built around 550 B.C. in the Greek city of Ephesus to honor the goddess Artemis. All marble, it was one of the most complicated temples ever built in ancient times. It had 127 columns, each 60 feet high.

# OF THE ANCIENT WORLD?

**The Statue of Zeus** was built around 435 B.C. in Olympia, Greece. Zeus was the king of the gods in ancient Greece—and this statue fit his role. It was said to be 40 feet high. Zeus was carved in ivory sitting on his throne in royal robes made of gold.

**The Colossus of Rhodes** was a huge bronze statue in the city of Rhodes in ancient Greece. It was built to honor Helios, the sun god. It took 12 years to complete and was probably 120 feet tall, about the same size as the Statue of Liberty. In 224 B.C., the statue was destroyed by an earthquake.

The **Lighthouse of Alexandria** was on the island of Pharos in the harbor of Alexandria, Egypt. Built in 270 B.C., it was said to be more than 440 feet high, square on the bottom, eight-sided in the middle, and circular on top—where a fire burned to guide ships at night.

**The Mausoleum at Halicarnassus** was built around 353 B.C. in what is now Turkey. The marble tomb was constructed for Mausolus, an official of the Persian Empire. The tomb became so famous that large tombs are now called *mausoleums*.

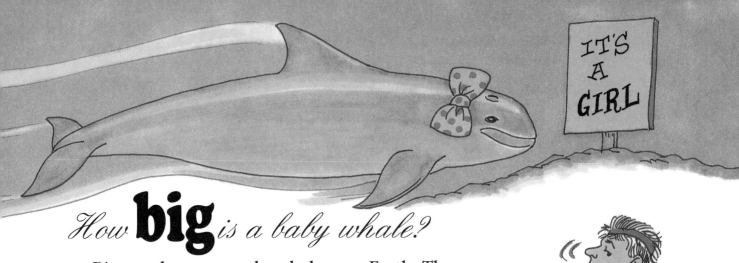

## *How* **big** *is a baby whale?*

Bigger than any other baby on Earth. The largest whale is the blue whale and its baby is the biggest. At birth, these babies can be 20 to 26 feet long and weigh more than 6,000 pounds. Just one year later they can grow to 28 tons!

## HOW DOES A REMOTE CONTROL WORK?

Invisibly—with infrared light rays and electricity. If you want to change the channel on your TV, you press a button on the remote control unit and send a beam of infrared rays to the receiver unit in the TV. The beam contains a signal made up of electrical pulses. The receiver detects the signal. Then it "decodes" the signal and changes the channel.

## WHO INVENTED CHEWING GUM?

The stuff of "chewing" gum is chicle (CHEE-clay), the gum of the sapodilla tree. The Aztec Indians of Mexico chewed it to clean their teeth. In 1872, Thomas Adams mixed sugar and flavor with chicle and created a rubbery candy. Actually, he was looking for a substitute for rubber when he popped a piece of chicle into his mouth. He chewed on his idea for a while and out popped gum!

# HOW DOES HAIL FORM?

A hailstone forms when a drop of moisture from a cloud gets tossed in the wind. An "updraft" catches the drop and swings it upward where the temperature is below freezing. The drop freezes, then falls into the cloud again. It's blown back up. Another layer of ice is added. This ping-pong effect can go on and on until an ice pellet is heavy enough to plunge to the ground. Huge hailstones can smash roofs, break windows, and even harm people. One hailstone that fell to Earth weighed two and a half pounds!

OUCH!

## Does it hurt a woodpecker to hammer on a tree?

No. Woodpeckers are hard-headed. They have thick skulls that can take the banging, and strong neck muscles that absorb the shock. Woodpeckers drill holes to get at the insects inside trees.

OH, NO! HAIL!!

## What makes a flower smell good?

All plants and animals have characteristics or behaviors that help them reproduce. In order to grow seeds, flowers must transfer pollen from their male parts to their female parts. Insects often carry the pollen. And flowers attract the insects with their smells. The perfume comes from tiny particles called scent strips on the petals and other parts of the flower.

# When did women first compete in sports?

For most of history, the two words "women" and "sports" didn't go together. But the world is constantly changing. Women first competed in the Olympic Games in golf and tennis in 1900. They wore long skirts, which certainly didn't help their games. As time went on, women began competing in almost all the sports that men have been playing for centuries.

## HOW DOES A TADPOLE TURN INTO A FROG?

*Metamorphosis* (met-ah-MORE-foh-sis). That's the big word for change in an animal's body. Frogs begin life as tadpoles—tiny, tailed, fishlike creatures that breathe with gills in the water. As tadpoles grow, rear legs appear, then front legs. Then the tail disappears and the creature *looks* like a frog. But it is not until lungs replace the gills that the tadpole *becomes* a frog—an animal that breathes air on land. Some frogs metamorphose in days or weeks. The big, noisy bullfrog takes nearly a year.

## WHAT IS VIRTUAL REALITY?

Reality is reading this book. Or sitting in a chair. Or anything that happens to you. Virtual Reality (VR, for short) is not real life, but it can be close. People create VR with computers. They feed the computer information. The computer turns the facts into visual images that behave and move as if they were real. To "feel" the virtual world, you might wear a headset or goggles, a computerized vest, or a pair of gloves. Your chair might be attached to the computer. If you were on a roller coaster in virtual reality, you would feel the sensations of the ride. You would be plunged into a new "unreal" reality.

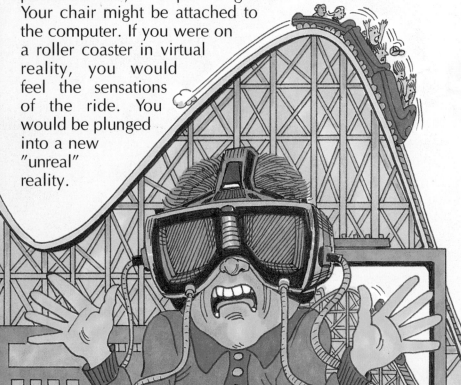

# DO ANY REAL HAUNTED HOUSES EXIST?

It's spooky, but many people think they do. The Winchester House in California is a big house actually built for ghosts. Sarah Winchester, heiress to the Winchester rifle fortune, was told by a psychic that a curse had been placed on her by the ghosts of people killed by the rifles. To get rid of the curse, the psychic told Sarah to build a house for the spirits. At the end of 38 years the house had 160 rooms and 950 doors! In her will, Sarah insisted that ghosts always be welcomed there. Want to visit?

WE'LL TAKE IT!

FOR RENT

## WHAT MAKES SPECIAL EFFECTS ON TV AND IN THE MOVIES SO REAL?

PUFF!

Cinematography. Camera techniques used in movies create illusions—scenes that look real, but are not. One technique is "rear screen projection." A separate film is shown behind the actors so they appear to be in a scene, but they really aren't. Another trick is to film tiny figures so that they look life-size. Imagine a doll-size plastic dragon and a model boat in a bucket of water. Look again. The camera makes it seem like a monster rising out of the ocean to attack a ship. That's entertainment!

# What are feathers made of?

Keratin, a protein, the same substance that you have in your hair and nails. Feathers on a bird are called plumage, and they can be beautiful colors—red, yellow, brown, even blue and violet. But they're not just for decoration. Feathers are for flying.

## HOW DO I REMEMBER THINGS?

Think of your brain as a gigantic computer, but much more complicated. Nerve cells take in information and pass it back and forth. Suppose you eat a peach for the first time. Nerves in your eyes, nose, and mouth pass along news to your brain about how a peach looks, smells, and tastes. Your brain records the word "peach" and the experience of eating it. The next time you think of a peach your brain will call up the stored information.

# Who invented chess?

The earliest recorded chess games were played in Persia about 1,500 years ago. The term "checkmate" comes from the Persian phrase *shah mat*, which means "the king cannot escape." The Arabs learned chess when they conquered Persia in the 7th century A.D., and then brought the game to Spain, from where it spread throughout Europe. International tournaments began in 1851.

I'M A KING!

I'M A QUEEN!

I'M A ROOK!

I'M A BISHOP!

I'M A KNIGHT!

I'M A PAWN!

## WHERE IS THE RING OF FIRE?

Where the volcanoes are. The Ring of Fire describes the area where more than 75 percent of the world's 850 active volcanoes are. The boundaries are where the earth's crust under the Pacific Ocean meets the continents. The "ring" goes from Alaska in North America to Chile in South America on one side and from Siberia to New Zealand on the other. The most volcanoes are in Indonesia—a very hot spot.

VOLCANO!

## HOW DOES A RADIO WORK?

Radio waves do the work. They are electromagnetic waves in the air that vibrate at different rates, or frequencies. Radio signals pass along these waves at incredible speeds, faster than the speed of light, nearly 190,000 miles per second. At the radio station, words or music are turned into electrical signals and sent from an antenna, along a radio wave frequency, to your radio. When you turn on that station's number, you are tuning into that frequency and receiving its signal.

VOLCANO!

21

# HOW MANY GALAXIES ARE IN THE UNIVERSE?

8 BILLION AND 2...
8 BILLION AND 3...
8 BILLION AND 4...

Billions—more than we can see with even the most powerful telescopes. Each galaxy is a huge collection of gas, dust, and, probably, billions of stars, all held together by gravity. The sun and its planets, including Earth, are part of a galaxy called the Milky Way. Look for a hazy band of bright stars across the night sky and you may see part of it.

## HOW IS A HOLOGRAM MADE?

PHOTOGRAPHIC PLATE

PHOTOGRAPHIC PLATE

With lasers, light, and mirrors that play tricks with our eyes. A hologram is really a flat image, but it looks three-dimensional. Special photographic film is used to develop the picture. First, an object is lit by a laser beam. One part of the beam reflects off the object onto the photographic plate. Another part of the beam reflects off mirrors onto the plate. When the plate is developed, it records the two images. Then, when we look at the picture in certain lights, it appears as if the image is three-dimensional and has depth.

# WHY DO WE BURP?

BURP!

EXCUSE ME!

It's the body's way of getting rid of the air we "eat." When you take a big gulp of food, you're treating your stomach to air along with it. When you drink a fizzy soda, those air-filled bubbles bounce around in your belly. Sometimes the entrance valve to the stomach opens and the air rushes up. It vibrates in the throat and makes the noise we call—excuse me—a burp.

# Who was the first African-American to play baseball in the major leagues?

Jackie Robinson, a real sports hero. When he began playing for the Brooklyn Dodgers in 1947, he was the only African-American in baseball. Unfortunately, there were still a lot of people who thought he didn't belong. But he stood up for what was right. He played for 10 years and helped his team win six National League pennants. In 1962, Jackie Robinson became the first African-American to enter the National Baseball Hall of Fame.

## WHAT IS DÉJÀ VU?

Have you ever been someplace for the first time but had the feeling you'd been there before? Have you ever met a stranger and felt like you'd met him or her before? This odd feeling is called déjà vu. The word comes from the French *déjà*, which means "already," plus *vu*, which means "seen."

# WHAT DO DIFFERENT COLORS SYMBOLIZE?

It depends where you are. Colors often have different meanings in different countries. For example, in the United States, red stands for danger—stop signs are red. And it symbolizes love—hearts are red. But it can also mean anger, as in "I saw red!" In China, however, red is the color of happiness. In the U.S., brides wear white to their weddings. In China, mourners wear white to funerals.

# WHO MADE THE FIRST MAP?

YOU ARE HERE X

Someone who wasn't going too far. The first known map was a clay tablet that shows a portion of the Euphrates River in Mesopotamia, which is now Iraq. That was around 2300 B.C. The most famous ancient maps were made by Claudius Ptolemy, an Egyptian scholar. Around A.D. 150 he drew a map of the world as it was known at that time. He included regional maps of Europe, Africa, and Asia. The whole Western Hemisphere was yet to be discovered. In other words, we weren't on the map.

## What was Mark Twain's real name?

Samuel Clemens. One of America's greatest writers, he lived from 1835 to 1910, and his books are just as much fun today as they were a century ago. Two of his stories, *The Adventures of Tom Sawyer* and *The Adventures of Huckleberry Finn*, are among the best-known novels in American fiction.

## WHEN WAS THE FIRST BOOK PRINTED?

The first book was "printed" in China in A.D. 868 with wooden blocks dipped in ink. Other wooden block systems were invented, but they were too slow and difficult to use to create many books. In 15th-century Germany, Johannes Gutenberg invented a way to print with metal blocks that moved around and could be used again and again. In 1455, with this first printing press, he produced copies of the Gutenberg Bible. For the first time, books were available to many people.

## HOW DO PICTURES AND SOUND GET ONTO MY TV SCREEN?

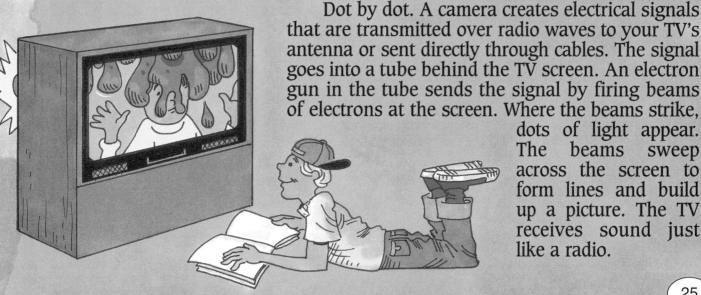

Dot by dot. A camera creates electrical signals that are transmitted over radio waves to your TV's antenna or sent directly through cables. The signal goes into a tube behind the TV screen. An electron gun in the tube sends the signal by firing beams of electrons at the screen. Where the beams strike, dots of light appear. The beams sweep across the screen to form lines and build up a picture. The TV receives sound just like a radio.

# What is the largest fish?

## What happens to the water I drink?

It goes to work. About half your blood is made up of water, which moves blood cells through your veins and arteries. Water also plays a big role in your organs. For example, water in your liver helps process digested foods. Water in your kidneys helps filter waste out of your blood. And water in your urine carries the waste out of your body. A grown man has 10 quarts of water circulating in his body every day.

## WHO INVENTED CHEESE?

Cheese is an ancient food. Experts believe it was first eaten in the Middle East. It seems likely that someone who raised cows, goats, or sheep first made cheese by accident. When milk sours it separates into curds (soft clumps), and whey (liquid). The curds can be aged into cheese. The Sumerians, a people that thrived 6,000 years ago in the area that is now Iraq, were probably the first cheese lovers.

The whale shark—a gentle giant you don't have to be afraid of (it only eats tiny sea creatures). One of the largest whale sharks ever captured was more than 40 feet long and weighed about 33,000 pounds. They may be big, but whale sharks are rarely seen.

# WHY DO THE DAYS GET LONGER AND SHORTER DURING THE YEAR?

We're spinning. Earth spins, or rotates, tilted on its *axis*, an imaginary line from the North Pole to the South Pole. Earth also makes a complete circle around the sun each year. These two motions constantly put us in a different position, relative to the sun. During part of the year, the North Pole tilts toward the sun, causing longer days in the Northern Hemisphere. When the South Pole tilts toward the sun, the Southern Hemisphere has longer days. But it happens gradually as Earth's position shifts. So each day the amount of light reaching your part of the world changes just slightly.

## Why did castles have moats?

It was one more way to keep enemies out! In the Middle Ages, landowners in Europe fought over their territory. These "land lords" built their castles as forts, with high stone walls for protection. But to keep enemies from climbing the walls, the castle was surrounded by a moat, a deep ditch usually filled with water. A moat was crossed by a drawbridge that could be raised from within the castle.

# What is an ENDANGERED animal?

If an animal species is close to extinction and there are so few left in the world, it is said to be endangered. An animal becomes endangered for many reasons. Pollution may ruin its territory. Cutting down forests may destroy its habitat. Hunting may wipe out its population. Chemicals may poison its food source. But people can make a big difference. In 1987, there were only 27 California Condors left. Conservationists captured and bred the rare birds in an attempt to recover their population. Through conservation efforts, many endangered animals have been rescued, including the bald eagle, the bison, and the American alligator.

## Why does it hurt to pull your hair but not to cut it?

The hair on your head is dead. Each hair starts growing below the skin in a follicle that contains a root. New cells in the root divide and force older cells upward. That's when the older hair cells die and harden into the hair you see on your head. The hair below the skin is alive and surrounded by nerves. Pull it and you'll feel it!

SNIP! SNIP! SNIP!

# What is the coldest place on Earth?

MOM DID TELL ME TO BUNDLE UP!

About 800 miles from the South Pole in Antarctica. That's where the lowest temperature has been recorded. In July 1983, on a day when you might have been swimming, the temperature in Vostok was -129°F. Don't even think about the windchill factor!

# What causes an avalanche?

The wind can trigger an avalanche, but so can melting snow, or a sudden loud sound like a rifle shot. The rest is all downhill—tons of snow, ice, mud, or rock crashing down a mountainside. The wind created by an avalanche can be enormous. In 1970, an avalanche in Peru swept through towns and villages, killing at least 18,000 people on its way.

FEET, DO YOUR THING!!

## Which famous composer of music was deaf?

Ludwig van Beethoven (1770-1827)—one of the greatest composers who ever lived. Even as a young German boy his talents were recognized by major artists. He began to lose his hearing at age 30, and his world was silent by age 47. But he kept right on composing, and left the world the gift of his music.

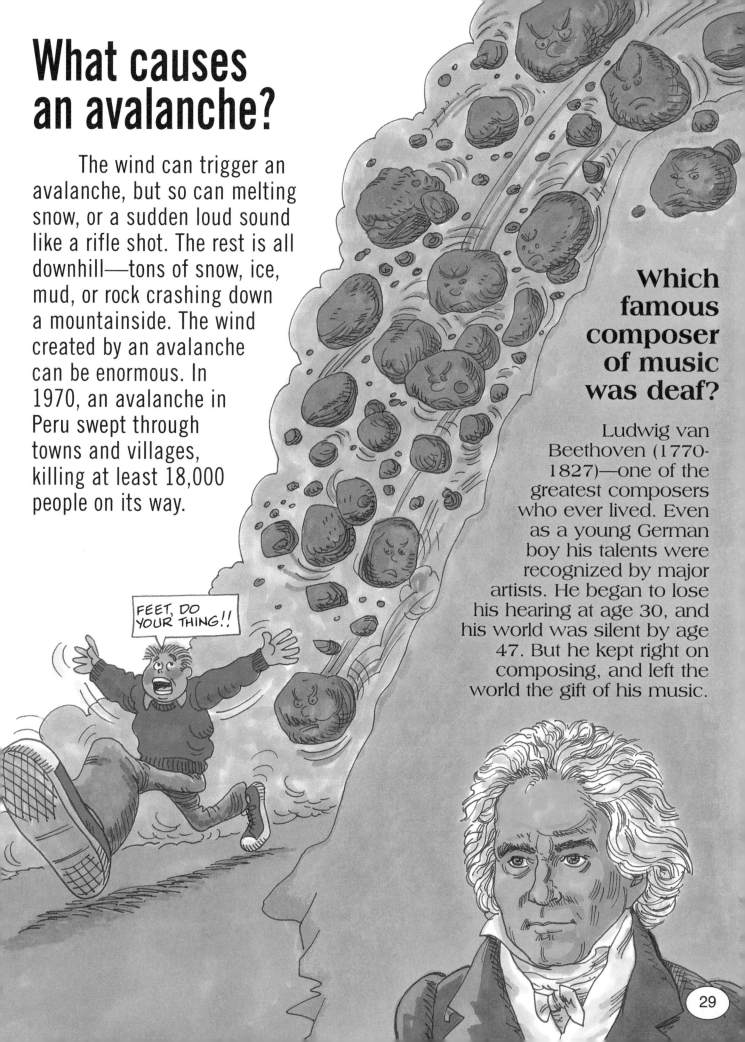

## WHAT DOES IT MEAN TO BE DOUBLE-JOINTED?

Nothing. Every elbow, knee, ankle, and shoulder is a spot where two bones meet and a joint connects them. Fingers and toes have many joints. Some people can bend these joints in pretty amazing ways. But they've got the same amount of joints as the rest of us. They're just more flexible.

# HOW DOES MY HEART WORK?

Automatically—and it never gets tired. Your heart is a powerful muscle that pumps blood around your body. It's made up of two types of muscle, *striated* (voluntary) and *smooth* (involuntary). Smooth muscle allows the heart to beat regularly. Blood travels through veins and arteries to and from your heart. Arteries carry oxygen-rich blood to every part of your body. Veins carry blood back to your heart to pick up more oxygen. As your heart does its job, the cycle occurs over and over again.

ARTERIES TO HEAD, ARMS, AND NECK

PULMONARY ARTERY

AORTA

SUPERIOR VENA CAVA

VALVE

LEFT ATRIUM

LEFT VENTRICLE

RIGHT PULMONARY VEINS

RIGHT ATRIUM

INFERIOR VENA CAVA

RIGHT VENTRICLE

SEPTUM

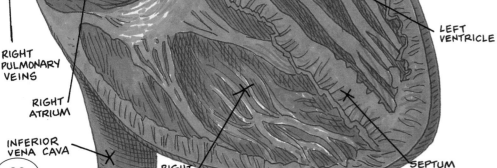

IT DOESN'T LOOK LIKE A HEART!

# Why do we blink?

To keep our eyes clean. Tear glands under our upper eyelids make tears all the time. When we blink, thousands of times a day, we spread the tears to wash away dust and dirt. Our eyelashes also keep things from entering our eyes. But we can also blink on purpose, as if to say "Just kidding!" That's called winking!

# WHY DO WE LAUGH ?

Because it feels good and helps us relax. What we laugh at is another story. You could giggle yourself silly over something that your friend thinks is stupid or boring or even insulting. But once you get started, it's hard to stop. Laughter is one of the automatic responses your body takes care of on its own. Your stomach tenses up. Your face scrunches up. Tears squeeze out of your tear glands. And when it's over, you feel good!

# How do we grow?

Slowly. Our pituitary gland, located at the bottom of the brain, sets the pace. One of the hormones, or chemicals, it releases stimulates growth, causing our cells to divide and multiply. The more cells there are, the more of us there is! Scientists aren't sure why we stop growing, but fortunately there seems to be a limit.

# What's the difference between a ROCK and a MINERAL?

A rock is solid material made up of minerals. A mineral forms from chemical combinations in the earth. Salt is one type of mineral. Minerals may be hard or soft, shiny or dull. They may be colorful, and they may conduct heat or electricity. Minerals in different combinations form different types of rocks. Marble, a very hard rock, and chalk, a soft powdery substance, both contain the same mineral—calcium carbonate.

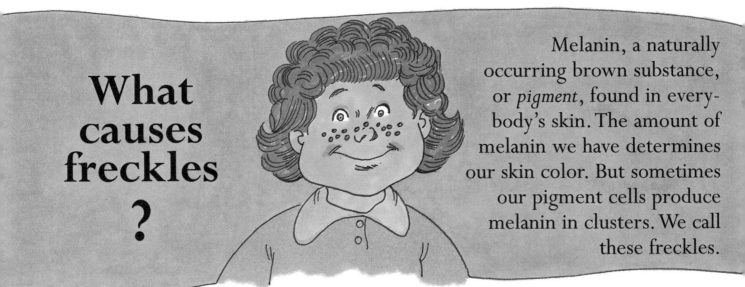

# What causes freckles ?

Melanin, a naturally occurring brown substance, or *pigment*, found in everybody's skin. The amount of melanin we have determines our skin color. But sometimes our pigment cells produce melanin in clusters. We call these freckles.

I WAS NAMED AFTER HIM!

# Who invented the teddy bear?

In 1902, President Teddy Roosevelt went hunting and refused to shoot a bear cub. A cartoonist drew a picture for a newspaper of the great president sparing the life of the little bear. Morris Michtom, a Brooklyn toy maker, thought the cartoon would help him sell stuffed bears. He was right. He put the bear in his window with the picture and called it "Teddy's Bear." Toys in America haven't been the same since. Presidents have come and gone, a century has passed, and the teddy bear is still going strong.

# WHERE DO PIÑATAS COME FROM?

South of the border, from Central and South America. Piñatas filled with candy or toys are now found at children's parties all over the world. Often made of papier-mâché in the shape of an animal, piñatas are colorfully decorated and hung from a rope. The idea is to whack the piñata open with a stick or a bat. Sometimes the children are blindfolded, so the treats that spill out are really a surprise.

## Do animals dream? Do babies?

Babies do, and they spend much more time dreaming than adults. One theory is that we dream to sort out new experiences, knitting them in with the rest of our lives. Babies have a new experience about every minute.

Animals, however, are a different matter. The brains of animals such as reptiles and fish are constructed much differently from ours, making them very difficult to study. But there have been experiments with other mammals, such as monkeys and cats, which seem to show that they dream. Just imagine if they could tell us what they dream about!

Because it's big—864,000 miles across—and it's HOT! The sun's core is hotter than you can imagine—about 30,000,000°F. *Thermonuclear* explosions, occurring at the sun's core, create heat and pressure that change hydrogen gas into helium. That process, called *fusion*, creates huge amounts of energy that burst to the surface, appearing as heat and light. This heat and light "shine" all the way to Earth, over 92 million miles away. It takes sunlight about eight minutes to get here.

AH! THAT FEELS GOOD!

I CAN'T EVEN FLY A KITE!

# What would it be like to live on the MOON?

You'd be trapped in a space suit because there's no oxygen to breathe. The temperature on the moon ranges from scorching hot, a sizzling 216°F, to the ultimate frozen zone, -279°F! And one cycle from day to night is 27 Earth days.

# How does a seed grow into a plant?

Germination—that's a big word for the sprouting of a seed. Seeds need the right temperature, moisture, and oxygen to germinate. First, water softens the seed coat, and the growing parts break out of the seed. A root grows downward. Then the stem bends upward and breaks through the soil. Small roots branch off the main root. Then the leaves develop and the plant is on its own.

# Who was King Midas?

In Greek mythology, the god Dionysus gave Midas the ability to turn everything he touched into gold. But there was one problem—even his food turned to gold. Luckily, Dionysus took back his blessing. But the memory of Midas lives on in this saying about successful people: "They have the Midas touch."

## WHAT HAPPENED DURING THE ICE AGES?

Ice covered large parts of the Earth. Scientists believe that ice ages occur every 150 million years or so due to changes in the global climate. During the last Ice Age, which ended about 10,000 years ago, parts of North America and Europe were covered with ice up to 9,800 feet thick! Glaciers, huge masses of moving ice, crushed forests, created mountains, and carved out valleys. As the global climate warmed, glaciers began to melt and receded toward the North and South Poles. Glaciers still exist in cold parts of the world, such as Greenland, Canada, and Antarctica.

# Who was Joan of Arc?

A French farm girl who became a saint by fighting for her country. Jeanne d'Arc (1412-1431) lived at a time when France was at war with England and losing badly. Jeanne had visions that convinced her she could liberate France. She persuaded the king to allow her to lead men into battle—imagine a 17-year-old girl in armor giving orders to generals! She recaptured the city of Orléans and became a great hero. In the end, she was captured by her enemies and burned at the stake as a witch. In 1920, the Roman Catholic Church declared her a saint.

## What's the difference between KARATE and TAE KWON DO?

Both are martial arts, Asian forms of unarmed combat. Karate developed in Okinawa, Japan, in the 17th century. Tae Kwon Do began in Korea around 50 B.C. Karate means "empty hand" and focuses on using the hands and arms. Tae Kwon Do means "the art of kicking and punching" and focuses more on leg power. Aside from self-defense and physical fitness, all martial arts set out to teach a way of life. Emphasis is on concentration, confidence, and harmony with nature. Fighting is the last option for solving a conflict in real life.

## Where is the world's longest roller

# IS EARTH THE ONLY PLANET THAT HAS A MOON?

Heavens, no! In our solar system nine planets circle the sun. Moons circle most of the planets—and that's many moons. Saturn has at least 22, and Jupiter at least 16. Uranus is right up there with at least 15 moons, and Neptune follows with 8 or more. Pluto has only one, but it's half the size of the planet. Only Mercury and Venus are out there alone.

## HOW DID THE LOST CONTINENT OF ATLANTIS GET LOST?

It may have never existed. The Greek philosopher Plato (427-347 B.C.) wrote a story about a glorious island in the Atlantic Ocean that sank into the sea because of earthquakes and floods. Although Plato never claimed his tale was true, some people came to believe that Atlantis really existed.

In a place where stomachs drop and fear rises—Lightwater Valley Theme Park in England. The roller coaster is called The Ultimate. And at 1.42 miles, it certainly is.

# How does a gasoline engine work?

A gasoline engine creates the force of energy that gets a vehicle going. *Combustion* is the key—a quick explosion that creates heat. This heat creates energy. In a car engine, a mixture of air and gasoline is lit by a spark in a *cylinder* containing a *piston*. (Think of a can with a disk-shaped plunger that fits exactly inside.) The heat from this little explosion makes the air expand and forces down the piston. The piston turns the *crankshaft*, a rod that is linked to the wheels. The wheels turn and off you go!

## How can penguins tell each other apart?

It's all beak speak. When thousands of look-alike penguins gather in the same place each year for mating, the males attract females by *calling*. Couples "sing" together to learn each other's unique voice. Next year, when they return, many penguins find their long-lost mates from the year before. Scientists believe they can recognize each other's voice.

# Who invented BASKETBALL?

I DID!

A Canadian, Dr. James Naismith. In 1891, as an instructor at the International YMCA Training School in Massachusetts, the idea struck him. It was December and too cold to play outdoor sports. The game he created had nine players to a team, and the "hoops" were wooden peach baskets. Four years later basketball was played everywhere in the country. Now it's played practically everywhere in the world.

## WHY DO I YAWN WHEN I GET SLEEPY?

To keep yourself up! A yawn is a slow, deep breath that brings more oxygen to the brain. It's a little like splashing cold water on your face. The oxygen gives your brain cells a little wake-up call.

## WHAT'S THE HOTTEST SPICE IN THE WORLD?

It's a type of chile—the Red "Savina" habanero. And it's *hot, hot, hot*! The tiniest bit can be tasted in over 700 pounds of mild sauce. Can I have a barrel of icewater with that, please?

# How come it never SNOWS in some places?

It never gets cold enough. To stay frozen, snowflakes must remain in a cold temperature on their fall to the earth. In some spots, especially those closest to the equator, the climate is always warm. However, even in warm areas, as you go up from the earth's surface, the temperature gets colder and colder. For example, Mount Kilimanjaro, the highest mountain in Africa, is just south of the equator—but its top is covered with snow.

I'LL PUT THE TV ROOM HERE!

LODGE PLANS

## Why do beavers build dams?

They're building a home. The amazing beaver "lodge" is a marvel of animal architecture. Beavers begin by cutting down trees with their sharp front teeth and powerful jaws. They use the tree trunks to build a watertight dam in a pond or lake. The dam is used to decrease the water level and to widen their living space. Then they build a room with rocks and twigs plastered together with mud. There's even a hole in the floor leading to the pond. Inside, beavers sleep and raise families.

WHAT'S THE RUSH?

BOOM!

40

# WHAT WILL CARS BE LIKE IN THE FUTURE?

They will be your driving partners. Get into the car and say "Good morning," and the seats and mirrors will adjust for you. Tell the car "Sorting mode," and it will get ready to rumble on country roads. If it rains, the windshield wipers will go on automatically. If you're too close to an object, the car will put on its brakes. A car that can help prevent accidents is really something to look forward to.

## If your skin is always renewing itself, how can you have a scar for life?

Your skin is like a rug woven of many fibers. If a cut isn't too wide, skin cells reweave the rug just like new. But if the cut edges are far apart, skin cells can't bridge the gap. Fibroblasts, cells that make bigger, tougher strands of skin, fill the space. This becomes a permanent scar.

# WHAT'S A SONIC BOOM?

A thunderous noise that occurs when an airplane flies faster than the speed of sound—about 760 miles per hour. When a jet plane breaks through the sound barrier, it presses against the air in front of and beside it. After the jet passes, the air expands again. The air molecules expand so fast that they collide with each other. This collision creates a BOOM and powerful shock waves that could shatter glass.

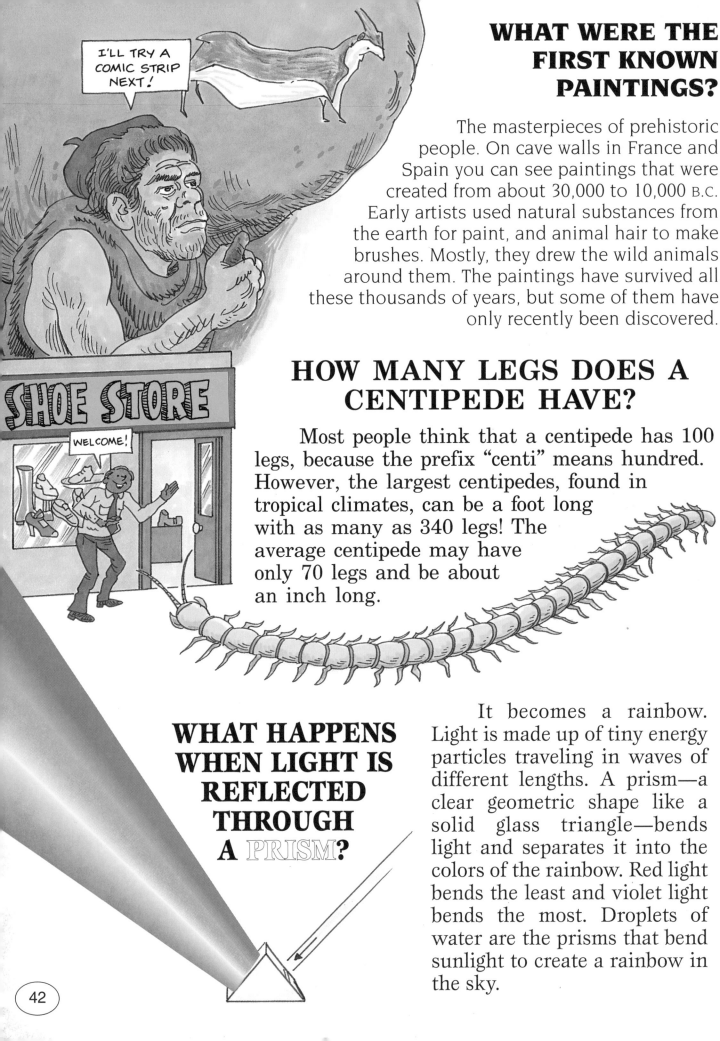

## WHAT WERE THE FIRST KNOWN PAINTINGS?

The masterpieces of prehistoric people. On cave walls in France and Spain you can see paintings that were created from about 30,000 to 10,000 B.C. Early artists used natural substances from the earth for paint, and animal hair to make brushes. Mostly, they drew the wild animals around them. The paintings have survived all these thousands of years, but some of them have only recently been discovered.

## HOW MANY LEGS DOES A CENTIPEDE HAVE?

Most people think that a centipede has 100 legs, because the prefix "centi" means hundred. However, the largest centipedes, found in tropical climates, can be a foot long with as many as 340 legs! The average centipede may have only 70 legs and be about an inch long.

## WHAT HAPPENS WHEN LIGHT IS REFLECTED THROUGH A PRISM?

It becomes a rainbow. Light is made up of tiny energy particles traveling in waves of different lengths. A prism—a clear geometric shape like a solid glass triangle—bends light and separates it into the colors of the rainbow. Red light bends the least and violet light bends the most. Droplets of water are the prisms that bend sunlight to create a rainbow in the sky.

# When were plays first performed?

The earliest known plays were performed in Athens, Greece, around the sixth century B.C. They were part of a spring festival honoring the Greek god Dionysus.

Plays were also performed in ancient Egypt more than 5,000 years ago.

I FORGOT THE WORDS!

Who invented **VIDEO GAMES?**

ZAP!

YUM!

POW!

The original video games seem pretty primitive compared to today's screen action. The first video game, invented in the 1970s by Nolan Bushnell, was a screen version of Ping-Pong called "Pong." At first, it was played only in arcades. Bushnell went on to develop Atari, the first successful home video system. Then Pac-Man came chomping along and was a huge success. Today's sophisticated video games, most of which can be played on a computer, are much more challenging and look like cartoons!

# HOW CAN WATER CREATE ELECTRICITY?

The force of falling water over a dam can power machines that make electricity. Here's how it works. Water falls from a great height onto the paddles of a turbine—think of a pinwheel spinning when you blow on it. These giant metal turbines whirl up to 750 revolutions per minute. They provide the mechanical energy that rotates the magnet in an electric generator. The generator uses magnets and copper wires to create electrical energy. This electricity travels through wires to the lightbulb on your desk.

WOW! COOL!!

# Are all snakes POISONOUS?

No. Snakes have a bad reputation because of the few poisonous ones. Of the 2,700 snake species, only about 400 are poisonous. Fewer than 50 kinds are dangerous to people. Most snakes will avoid people if at all possible. And most people will avoid snakes! The anaconda, weighing up to 400 pounds, is not poisonous but can squeeze the life out of a crocodile.

YOU RATTLE ME!

LET ME GIVE YOU A HUG!

RATTLE!

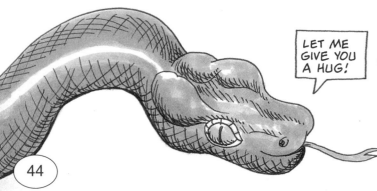

# WHY DO BABY TEETH FALL OUT?

They need to be replaced by bigger, stronger adult teeth. As you get bigger, your mouth grows. Soon, baby teeth no longer fit. When an adult tooth is ready to come in, it releases a chemical that dissolves the roots of the baby tooth it will replace. Without roots, the tooth is no longer anchored to the jawbone. It loosens and falls out—or gets pulled out!

## How did the tooth fairy legend start?

Dr. Rosemary Wells, who's been researching the tooth fairy for more than 20 years, says that losing baby teeth has been important in all cultures, even ancient ones. It's a symbol of "leaving babyhood and entering childhood." Some countries have invented magical animals instead of a fairy. The United States is the only country with a tooth fairy who exchanges money for teeth! Dr. Wells has a Tooth Fairy Museum in Illinois with all kinds of objects, even a singing tooth fairy toothbrush.

# WHO WAS THE FIRST WOMAN IN SPACE ?

I'M VALENTINA TERESHKOVA.

I'M SALLY RIDE

In June of 1963, Valentina Tereshkova of the former Soviet Union became the first woman in space. She spent 71 hours aboard Vostok 6. Sally Ride was the first American woman in space. An astrophysicist from California, Sally made her historic journey in 1983.

# Why does poison ivy make people itch?

There's no poison in poison ivy, just an oil on the leaf that really clings to the skin. Your skin cells may detect this oil as an enemy. The cells rush to your defense, releasing chemicals that cause your skin to redden and blister, and ooze and itch, while they fight off the invader.

# How did the black widow spider get its name?

By her nasty reputation. The black widow is a female spider that often eats the male she mates with! So when she kills her "husband," she becomes a "widow"— and a wicked one at that. Her venom is 15 times stronger than a rattlesnake's!

**HOW DOES HYPNOTISM WORK?**

Basically, your mind works on two levels. The one you are aware of is your thinking, *conscious* mind. The one you aren't aware of is your *subconscious* mind, which stores up memories, dreams, and hidden feelings. A hypnotist guides you to your subconscious mind by helping you become totally relaxed. Most techniques direct you to focus your thoughts on one thing. When you're hypnotized you are not asleep. You can be aware of everything going on around you, but you stay focused. It's a type of concentration similar to daydreaming in class. You get so caught up in your own mind that you don't hear the sounds of your teacher or classmates. Sometimes this state is called a trance.

# WHY DOES JUMBO MEAN BIG?

Jumbo was an elephant who got his name from one of the most famous showmen who ever lived, P.T. Barnum (1810-1891), founder of the Barnum & Bailey Circus. Barnum was a man who knew how to capture an audience. His elephant was big—11 feet tall and 6½ tons—and his catchy name made him so famous that "jumbo" came to mean huge, gigantic, enormous, or just plain large. We can thank Jumbo, who died in 1885, for a very modern phrase—the jumbo jet.

# WHAT IS THE WORLD'S TALLEST STATUE?

A 394-foot statue of Buddha in Tokyo, Japan. Buddha, who lived from about 563 to 483 B.C., founded Buddhism, one of the great Asian religions. The bronze statue that honors him is 115 feet wide, and as tall as a 40-story skyscraper. The statue took seven years to build, and was finally completed in 1993.

47

# What is the largest lizard?

A lizard so large it's called a dragon—the Komodo dragon. This very scary creature can be 10 feet long and weigh 300 pounds. Its favorite meal is goat, and it has been known to attack humans. As a matter of fact, the Komodo dragon doesn't even have to bite to cause harm. Its saliva is so deadly that a good spray could do the trick. There are not many Komodo dragons in the world and they all live on a few small islands in Indonesia.

KISS ME!

# WHO INVENTED CHOCOLATE CHIP COOKIES?

Thank the cooks at a country inn in Whitman, Massachusetts. Around 1930, they put together a recipe combining bits of chocolate with cookie dough. The cookie was crunchy, buttery, and it tasted like candy, too! The combination is so simple and delicious that it's amazing no one ever thought of it before.

YUM!

YUM!

COOKIE!

ANY AGE LIKES THEM!

GO FOR IT!

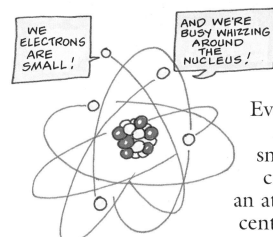

# Is there anything smaller than an atom?

Yes—the particles that make up an atom. Everything is made of atoms, including you and the chair you're sitting on. But they're so small—maybe a millionth of an inch—that they can be seen only with special microscopes. But an atom is made up of still smaller particles. At its center is a nucleus, which is 10,000 times smaller than the rest of the atom. And the nucleus is surrounded by electrons, which are even smaller!

## WHAT MAKES MY STOMACH GROWL?

It's telling you it wants food to digest! Digestion happens automatically. When your stomach is empty its muscles still contract, as if it's looking for food. The walls squeeze together, creating the noises you hear. Digestive juices and acids roll around—rumbling, grumbling, and growling.

## What is sleepwalking?

Walking in your sleep, without any idea that you're moving. Sleepwalkers commonly perform actions such as looking for lost objects or trying to solve other problems. But we don't know too much more than that. You might think that sleepwalking and dreaming go together, but they don't. Experiments show that sleepwalking occurs during very deep sleep. Dreaming occurs during light sleep.

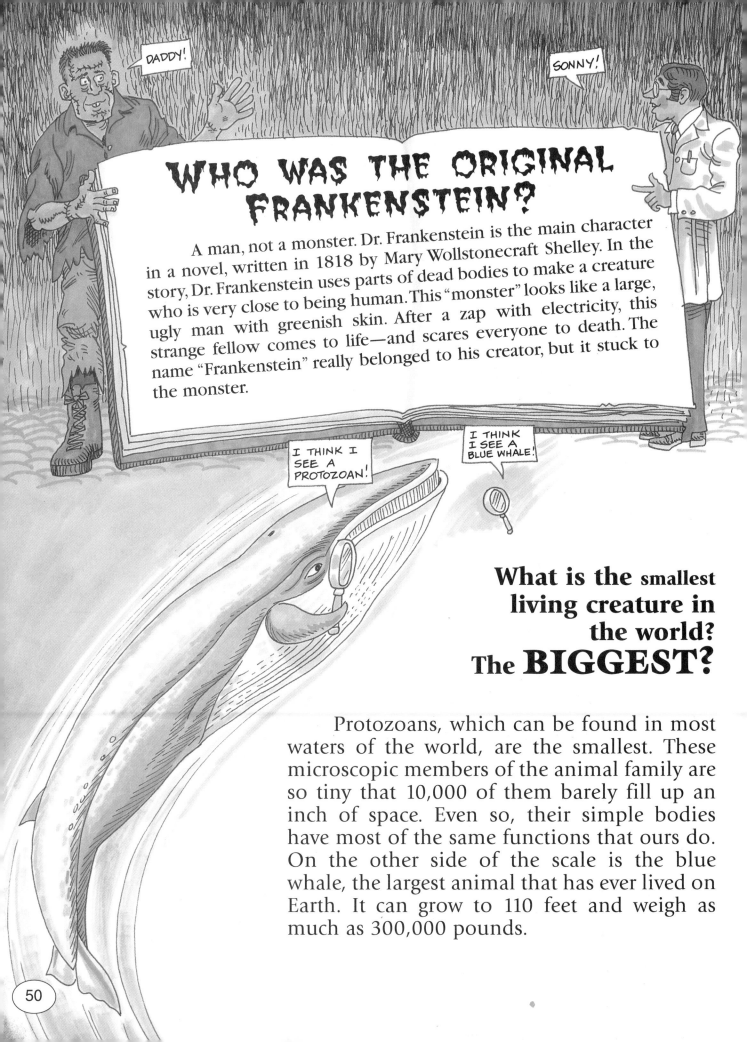

## WHO WAS THE ORIGINAL FRANKENSTEIN?

DADDY!

SONNY!

A man, not a monster. Dr. Frankenstein is the main character in a novel, written in 1818 by Mary Wollstonecraft Shelley. In the story, Dr. Frankenstein uses parts of dead bodies to make a creature who is very close to being human. This "monster" looks like a large, ugly man with greenish skin. After a zap with electricity, this strange fellow comes to life—and scares everyone to death. The name "Frankenstein" really belonged to his creator, but it stuck to the monster.

I THINK I SEE A PROTOZOAN!

I THINK I SEE A BLUE WHALE!

## What is the smallest living creature in the world? The BIGGEST?

Protozoans, which can be found in most waters of the world, are the smallest. These microscopic members of the animal family are so tiny that 10,000 of them barely fill up an inch of space. Even so, their simple bodies have most of the same functions that ours do. On the other side of the scale is the blue whale, the largest animal that has ever lived on Earth. It can grow to 110 feet and weigh as much as 300,000 pounds.

# How do meteorologists predict the weather?

They start with the world and then concentrate on your neighborhood.

First, they look at the big picture. Thousands of weather stations around the world measure temperature, humidity, air pressure, and wind direction. Weather balloons and satellites also provide information.

Next, computer programs take all these numbers and predict how world weather conditions are likely to move and change.

Finally, meteorologists consider all these facts and make a good guess about what will happen where you live.

# What is D-Day?

D-Day is the code name for the first day of a planned military attack. But World War II gave the name special meaning. During that war, Germany held France. But on D-Day, June 6, 1944, American, British, and other Allied soldiers attacked the Germans on the beaches of Normandy in France. That day was the beginning of the end for Germany, which surrendered less than a year later.

# Why do eyes sometimes look **RED** in photos?

When a camera flash is pointed directly into your eyes, the light travels through your pupils. The camera actually takes a picture of the insides of your eyes. There are so many blood vessels in your eyes that the camera sees red.

51

# What happens when water FREEZES?

Ice happens. Temperature affects the way molecules, the microscopic "building blocks" of a substance, bind together. At room temperature, water molecules are loosely connected. That's why water flows. But as the temperature drops to 32°F, water molecules slowly bind together until ice is formed.

**HARD WATER!**

## What was the world's first instrument?

Scientists discovered a piece of animal bone that may have been part of an ancient flute. Amazingly, the holes seem to be spaced in such a way that they play part of the musical scale we know today. Experts guess the bone instrument is 43,000 to 82,000 years old. It was found in a region once inhabited by the Neanderthals, an early human species. So it seems that *do, re, mi* has been around for a long, long time.

**LET'S SIGN HIM UP FOR OUR ROCK BAND!**

## WHY DO MY EARS POP IN AN AIRPLANE?

CAPTAIN, I JUST HEARD A POP!

It's in the air. Your eardrum is in its normal position when the air pressure is the same inside and outside your ear. When an airplane goes up or down, the air pressure outside the plane changes. The pilot must adjust the pressure inside the plane. This quick change in air pressure may cause a bulge in your eardrum. When the air pressure becomes equal again, your eardrum "pops" back into place.

**How many people have lived in the world since humans came to exist?**

About fifty billion is the best guess, and the number is increasing. Every minute, approximately 160 babies are born around the world.

## Where did bullfighting begin?

Even though bullfighting was known 4,000 years ago on the Greek island of Crete, Spain is the name to know when it comes to bulls and fighting. The Moors, Arabs who once ruled Spain, began the sport in the 11th century. Today bullfighting is still popular in Spain, Portugal, Mexico, and parts of South America.

THAT'S A LOT OF BULL!

53

IT'S MINE... ALL MINE!!

## Who was Genghis Khan?

A man with a plan to conquer the whole world. Genghis Khan (1167-1227), originally named Temüjin, was a Mongolian leader who came to power at only 13 years of age. The young ruler soon became known as Genghis Khan—"precious warrior." He united the Mongol tribes into a fierce fighting force. They invaded what is now China, Russia, Iran, and northwest India, creating one of the greatest empires of all time. Upon Genghis Khan's death, the Mongol Empire was divided among his three sons and gradually dissolved.

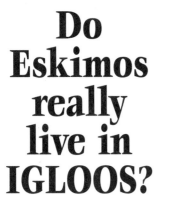

MUST SELL BEFORE SUMMER

## Do Eskimos really live in IGLOOS?

Not anymore. Igloos, or snow houses, were once used by Eskimos as temporary shelter when they traveled. Blocks of hard-packed snow or ice, about three feet long and two feet wide, were stacked in circles to form a dome-shaped house. Cozy on the inside, igloos were lit and heated by lamps that burned oil made from the blubber of sea mammals.

## Why do monkeys and apes groom each other?

Why do humans shake hands or give hugs? Touching is a form of communication. A social act, grooming helps to keep a group of monkeys together. Grooming is also symbolic of a monkey's social status. A monkey grooms those with a higher social position and is groomed by those of lower rank. Above all, grooming keeps monkeys clean!

54

# What is the Concorde?

WAIT FOR ME!!

The fastest way to travel. Instead of seven hours in the air from New York to Paris, the Concorde can get you there in three! The Concorde is the first supersonic passenger jet. It travels at more than 1,000 miles an hour. A British-French partnership put the plane into service in 1976. However, there aren't many Concordes flying around. This type of plane is still too expensive to make and keep up!

## What would happen if there were no more plants in the world?

ULP!

## Do stars last forever?

Not much could happen. Plants are a necessary link in the cycle of nature that connects all living things. *Photosynthesis*, the process by which plants use sunlight to make their own food, supplies us with the oxygen we breathe. Plants are a source of food and shelter for many animals. Plants also keep the soil from blowing away in the wind. There would be no world as we know it without plants.

No. Stars are mostly made up of hydrogen gas, which they are constantly burning. That's why stars shine. Eventually, they burn themselves up and explode, or simply burn out. How long that takes depends on the star. Giant stars, bigger than our sun, actually burn out quicker than smaller stars. Scientists believe our sun has been burning for five billion years—and it has five billion more to go. That's a long time, but it's not forever.

Larissa Latynina, a gymnast from the former Soviet Union, won 18 Olympic medals in all—9 gold, 5 silver, and 4 bronze. That's the most medals for an athlete in any sport. Amazingly, she did it in just 3 years—1956, 1960, and 1964. The women gymnastics stars that followed made the sport popular, but Larissa started it all.

# HOW DOES SOMETHING BECOME RADIOACTIVE?

Atoms are the tiny "building blocks" of all substances. Atoms contain energy. Over time, the *nucleus*, or center, of every atom decays. When this happens, parts of the atom shoot out in high-energy rays. This is called nuclear radiation, or radioactivity. When something is radioactive it becomes electrically charged. Most radioactive rays are too weak to harm us, but strong rays can be dangerous. Radioactivity is helpful for scientists who do medical research or study the Earth.

# What is the most common name on the planet?

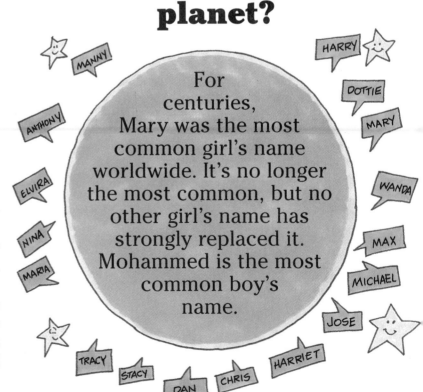

For centuries, Mary was the most common girl's name worldwide. It's no longer the most common, but no other girl's name has strongly replaced it. Mohammed is the most common boy's name.

# How much BLOOD is in my body?

HE USED HIS NOODLE!

# WHO CREATED SPAGHETTI?

The legend says that Italian explorer Marco Polo brought spaghetti back from China in 1292. However, carvings in a 5,000-year-old tomb near Rome show all the tools needed to make pasta. So who did it first—China or Italy? We may never know, but there is general agreement that Naples, Italy, is the birthplace of spaghetti as we know it today.

DID SOMEBODY SAY *BLOOD*?

I'D RATHER HAVE PASTA!

VENICE

CHINA

A grown-up has about 5 quarts of blood in his or her body. That means you probably have about 3 or 4 quarts of blood in your body. There are 4 quarts in a gallon. To get an idea of how much that is, think of one big container of milk.

# WHO INVENTED THE JIGSAW PUZZLE?

An Englishman who wanted to teach a geography lesson. In 1767, John Silsbury carved a wooden map of England and divided it into counties. Each county was one piece. They fit around each other according to their location. Puzzles as we know them today were developed in the 20th century.

## What is PLASTIC made of?

I'M FAMOUS!

## How does a PIANO make sound when you press a key?

STRING

HAMMER

DAMPER

KEY

Each of a piano's 88 keys is attached to at least one steel wire string. Each string has a "hammer" that strikes it. Pressing a key causes the hammer to strike its string. When the string is struck, it vibrates and makes the sound you think of as a "note." All together, there are nearly 4,000 parts in the action of one piano. And with only ten fingers, you can make all this action happen.

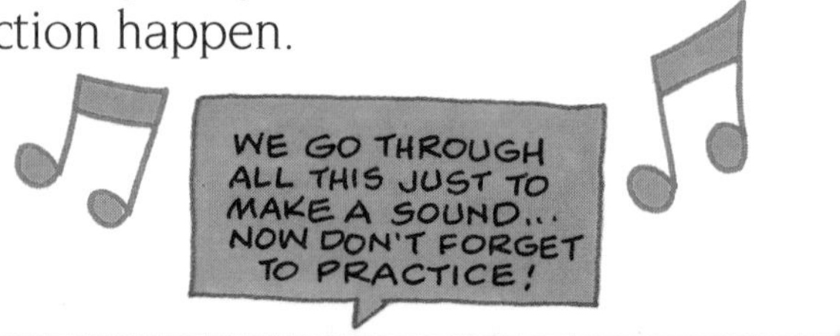

WE GO THROUGH ALL THIS JUST TO MAKE A SOUND... NOW DON'T FORGET TO PRACTICE!

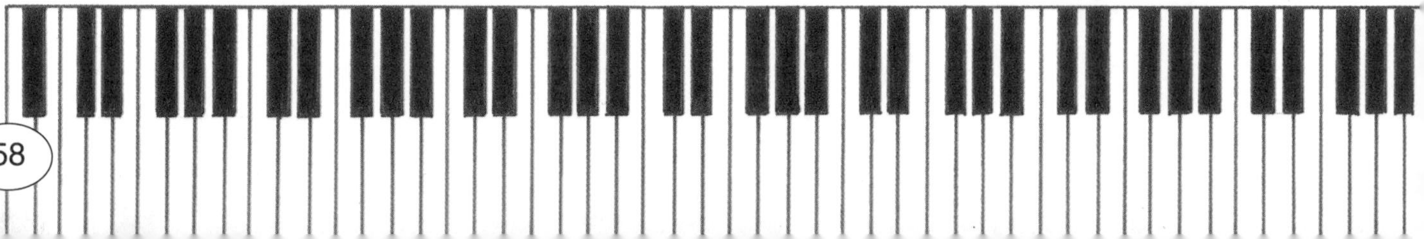

# Where is the Great Barrier Reef?

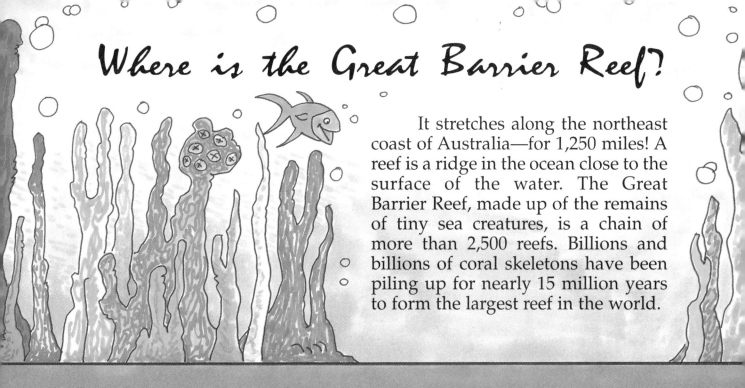

It stretches along the northeast coast of Australia—for 1,250 miles! A reef is a ridge in the ocean close to the surface of the water. The Great Barrier Reef, made up of the remains of tiny sea creatures, is a chain of more than 2,500 reefs. Billions and billions of coral skeletons have been piling up for nearly 15 million years to form the largest reef in the world.

Mixed-up oil molecules. Scientists discovered plastic by rearranging some of the molecules in oil. The process is called *polymerization*. Many *synthetic* (human-made) substances are created this way, including different kinds of plastic. The first useful plastic was celluloid, invented in 1870 by John Hyatt. It was used to make billiard balls. Maybe he liked to shoot pool!

# WHAT IS SPELUNKING?

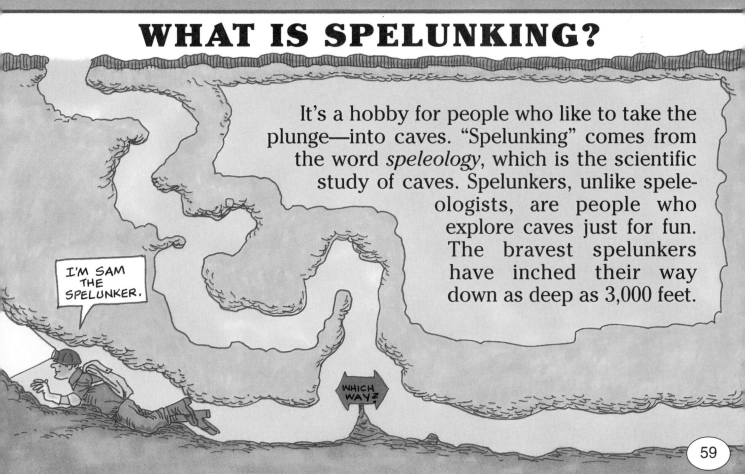

It's a hobby for people who like to take the plunge—into caves. "Spelunking" comes from the word *speleology*, which is the scientific study of caves. Spelunkers, unlike spele-ologists, are people who explore caves just for fun. The bravest spelunkers have inched their way down as deep as 3,000 feet.

# Who was AMELIA EARHART?

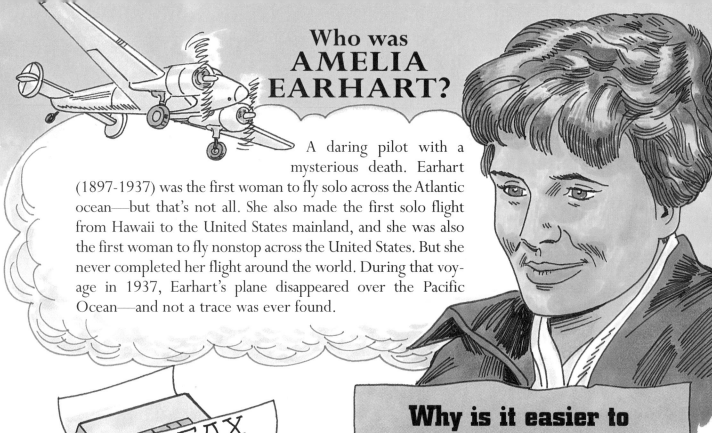

A daring pilot with a mysterious death. Earhart (1897-1937) was the first woman to fly solo across the Atlantic ocean—but that's not all. She also made the first solo flight from Hawaii to the United States mainland, and she was also the first woman to fly nonstop across the United States. But she never completed her flight around the world. During that voyage in 1937, Earhart's plane disappeared over the Pacific Ocean—and not a trace was ever found.

# HOW DOES A FAX MACHINE KNOW WHAT TO PRINT?

Electricity is used by the fax machine to "see" what it's printing. Fax is short for facsimile, which means a copy. When you send a fax, you send a copy of words or pictures to a fax machine at another location. A scanner in the fax machine "reads" the images by coding the dark areas in electrical signals. The signals travel over telephone wires. Finally, the printer in the receiving machine prints out the dark pattern in tiny dots, just the way your machine sent them.

# Why is it easier to balance on my bicycle when it's moving than when it's standing still?

A spinning wheel will stay upright on its own. This motion is called *precession*. You've seen it in a spinning top. The faster it spins, the longer the top stays up. As the spinning slows down, the top begins to wobble. The same goes for a bicycle wheel. The faster it spins, the more likely it is to stay up—and so are you!

THAT'S GREAT... BUT, I'M LOST!

# How does a thermometer work?

Heat and the metal mercury work together in a glass thermometer. A thermometer is a thin tube of glass with a hollow bulb at one end. The bulb is filled with mercury. When the mercury is heated, it expands and moves up the tube. The distance it moves is measured in degrees.

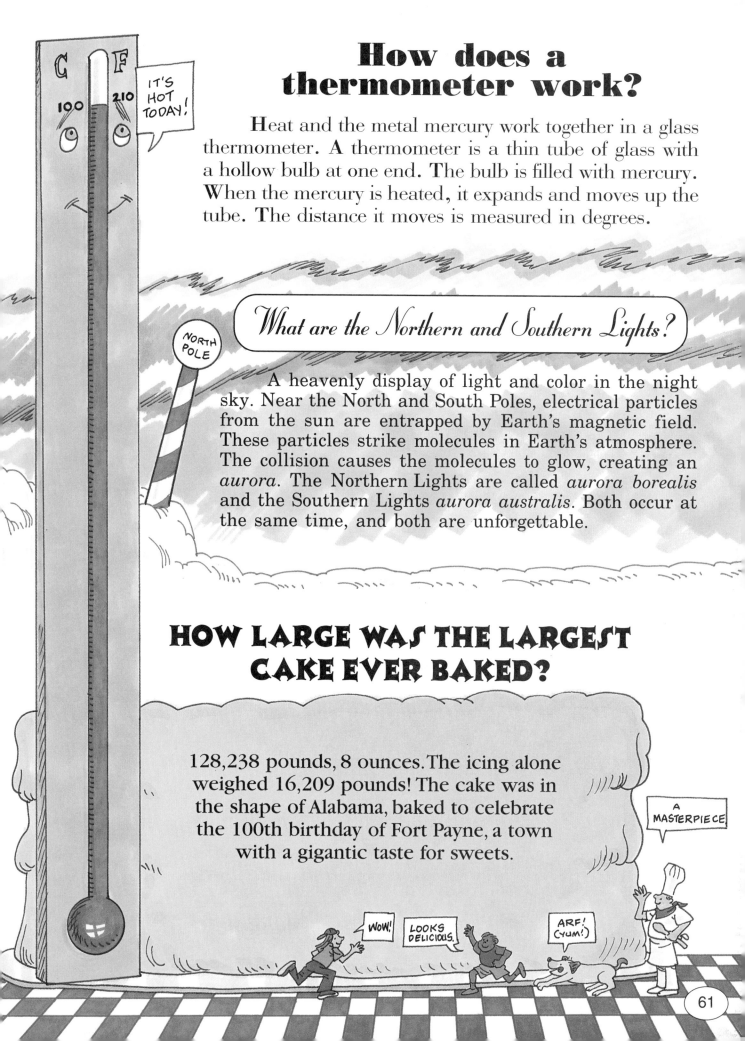

C F

100    210

IT'S HOT TODAY!

NORTH POLE

## What are the Northern and Southern Lights?

A heavenly display of light and color in the night sky. Near the North and South Poles, electrical particles from the sun are entrapped by Earth's magnetic field. These particles strike molecules in Earth's atmosphere. The collision causes the molecules to glow, creating an *aurora*. The Northern Lights are called *aurora borealis* and the Southern Lights *aurora australis*. Both occur at the same time, and both are unforgettable.

## HOW LARGE WAS THE LARGEST CAKE EVER BAKED?

128,238 pounds, 8 ounces. The icing alone weighed 16,209 pounds! The cake was in the shape of Alabama, baked to celebrate the 100th birthday of Fort Payne, a town with a gigantic taste for sweets.

A MASTERPIECE

WOW!

LOOKS DELICIOUS.

ARF! (YUM!)

# Why do we itch? Does scratching STOP an itch?

Itching and scratching seem simple, but they're mysterious. Scientists don't know exactly how to explain itching. We do know that certain sensations cause us to itch. For example, if an ant marched across your foot, it would itch. To stop the itching you would scratch. Scratching is a much more powerful sensation, so the itch seems to go away.

# What do Mars and Venus look like?

VENUS — I'M HOT!
I'M JUST RIGHT.
EARTH
THE MOON — I'M HOT AND COLD!
I'M COLD.
MARS

Mars is named for the Roman god of war because it looks bloodred. When space scientists took a closer look, they realized that the color is caused by rusted iron in the soil. The surface of Mars is covered by rocks and mountains. *Olympus Mons*, 16 miles high, is the tallest mountain in our solar system.

The rocky surface of Venus has large craters and high mountains. But the surface is difficult to see because the planet is surrounded by thick clouds. The clouds reflect and absorb sunlight, making Venus the hottest planet—over 800°F—and one of the brightest in our solar system.

# What are CRYSTALS made of?

Minerals are the basic elements of crystals. Crystals form when molten minerals, or minerals dissolved in heated liquid, cool. Each type of mineral forms crystals with particular shapes. For example, the mineral *galena*, the main source of lead, forms four-sided cubic crystals. Even though crystals are nonliving substances, they can "grow," or increase, by forming the same link over and over. This process is called *crystallization*.

# Who invented LANGUAGE?

No one knows for sure because there are certainly no written records of how words developed! Scholars think language may have begun around 3000 B.C., because the Sumerians of the Middle East invented writing around that time. This early form of writing, called *cuneiform* (kyu-NEE-uh-form), used symbols for whole words. The alphabet was invented in the Middle East around 1500 B.C. by the Phoenicians.

## Why doesn't it hurt a kitten when its mother picks it up by the scruff of its neck?

Kittens have plenty of loose skin around their neck, so the mother can get a good grip without pulling too hard. She hangs on to the skin but is careful not to bite. The kitten also cooperates by staying still. That way it's an easy, painless ride.

PUT ME DOWN MOM!

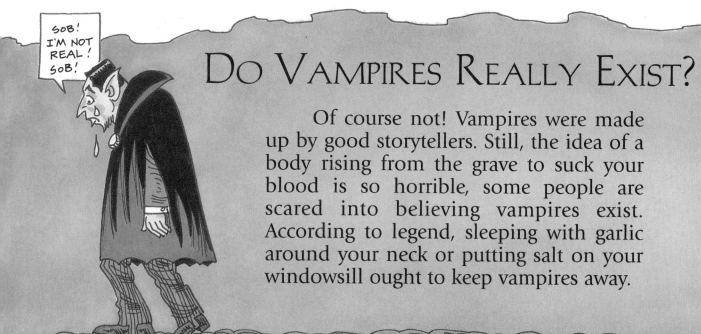

SOB! I'M NOT REAL! SOB!

# DO VAMPIRES REALLY EXIST?

Of course not! Vampires were made up by good storytellers. Still, the idea of a body rising from the grave to suck your blood is so horrible, some people are scared into believing vampires exist. According to legend, sleeping with garlic around your neck or putting salt on your windowsill ought to keep vampires away.

## Who are some of the most famous women leaders?

Women have held great power ever since Queen Hatshepsut ruled ancient Egypt around 1400 B.C. Cleopatra took the same role in 51 B.C. One of the most famous monarchs in history was Catherine the Great, Empress of Russia (1729-1796). Queen Victoria ruled the British Empire for more than 50 years. The 20th century has seen many more women leaders, including Indira Gandhi of India, Golda Meir as Prime Minister of Israel, and Margaret Thatcher, the first female Prime Minister of Great Britain.

GOOD SHOW, MAGGIE!

CLEOPATRA

#1

MARGARET THATCHER

## What's the difference between honeybees and wasps?

They belong to the same family, *Apoidea*, but there are many differences. Honeybees live in hives. Some wasps build a nest out of "paper," which they make by chewing on wood and passing it through their body. Another difference is that honeybees collect the sweet nectar from flowers to make honey. Wasps make a meal of other insects. Also, if a honeybee stings, it loses its stinger and dies. Not the wasp. It stings and lives to sting again. But honeybees live through the winter. Wasps, alas, do not.

IF I STING YOU... I'M HISTORY!!

I HATE THE WINTER!

NILE RIVER

## Where is the longest river in the world? The deepest lake?

The Nile River, running through Egypt and Sudan in Africa, is the longest river in the world. It's about 4,160 miles long. The Amazon River, running through South America, comes close at about 4,000 miles. Siberia, in Russia, is home to the deepest lake, Lake Baykal. Its lowest point plunges more than a mile below the surface— 5,315 feet.

I LIVE HERE.

# HOW DOES A GLACIER FORM?

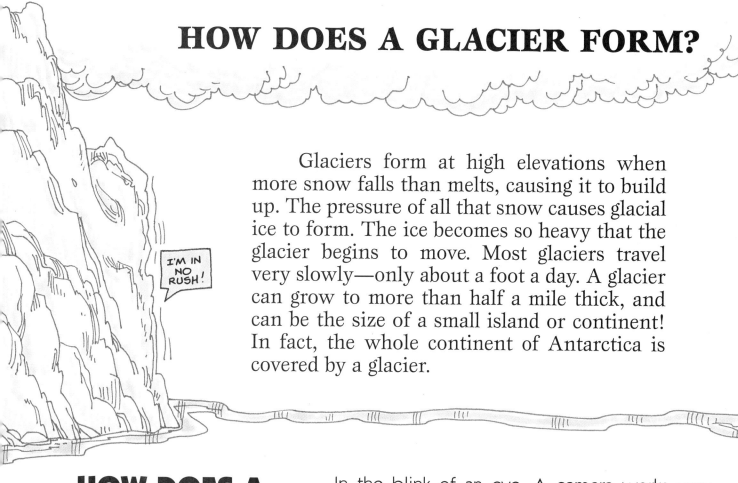

Glaciers form at high elevations when more snow falls than melts, causing it to build up. The pressure of all that snow causes glacial ice to form. The ice becomes so heavy that the glacier begins to move. Most glaciers travel very slowly—only about a foot a day. A glacier can grow to more than half a mile thick, and can be the size of a small island or continent! In fact, the whole continent of Antarctica is covered by a glacier.

I'M IN NO RUSH!

## HOW DOES A CAMERA WORK?

EVERYONE THAT'S LOOKING AT THIS PAGE SMILE!

In the blink of an eye. A camera works very quickly. Light only hits the film for a fraction of a second. The film, which records the picture, is very "light sensitive." When you take a picture, you look through the **view finder** and aim the camera. You press the button. The **shutter**, an opening and closing device, opens to let light in. The **lens** directs the light onto the film. Instantly, the shutter closes. Whatever the camera "saw" in that brief moment is what you get.

## What is the ozone layer?

It's part of Earth's atmosphere. As you go up from the ground, the gases that make up the atmosphere change. These "layers" of gas have different names. The ozone layer is about 12 to 30 miles above Earth's surface. Ozone is a form of oxygen that absorbs much of the sun's ultraviolet radiation and prevents it from reaching the ground. If this radiation did reach ground level, it would be harmful to most forms of life.

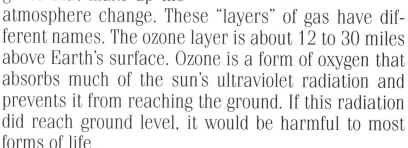

# How does water get to my sink?

It starts in a natural source like a lake, river, or reservoir. The water is pumped through pipes into large tanks. Fish, plants, and trash are screened out. Chemicals like chlorine are added to kill any bacteria or dangerous substances. If you live in a city, the water is then pumped into cast iron pipes called mains. The mains run beneath the streets and carry water to every hydrant, house, and building. The pumping station sends the water to every faucet. If you live in a rural area, water is pumped from a well right into your house. Turn it on!

TIME TO DRY OFF!

# WHAT IS A BRUISE?

I WALKED INTO A DOOR KNOB!

A bruise is a bunch of broken blood vessels beneath the skin. When they break, blood oozes out into the tissues around the spot. The tissues turn a purplish color. As the bruise heals, it changes into a rainbow of colors—first blue, then green, and finally yellow before it disappears. This happens as the blood is absorbed into the body again.

# Why do people eat turkey on Thanksgiving?

It has become a tradition. The first Thanksgiving in the New World was a celebration by the Pilgrims in 1621. It was an effort to thank the Native Americans who had helped the Pilgrims survive their first year. Our only real clue that they ate turkey is in a letter written by one of the men. It said the governor sent four men "fowling" for the feast. A turkey is a fowl—and there were plenty of wild turkeys roaming the woods in Massachusetts. Also, since Massasoit, the Indian chief, brought 90 braves for dinner, fat turkeys would have been very useful. By the early 1800s turkey became the Thanksgiving bird of America.

LET'S CHANGE IT TO HOT DOGS!

THAT'S NOT A GOOD IDEA!

# *What is the Nobel Prize?*

Annual awards given to people around the world who make "contributions to the good of humanity." Alfred Bernhard Nobel (1833-1896) was a Swedish chemist who invented dynamite and became extremely rich. He never got over the destruction his invention caused. Before he died, Nobel established a fund for prizes in physics, chemistry, medicine, literature, economics, and peace.

# WHAT ANIMAL HAS TEETH ALL OVER ITS BODY?

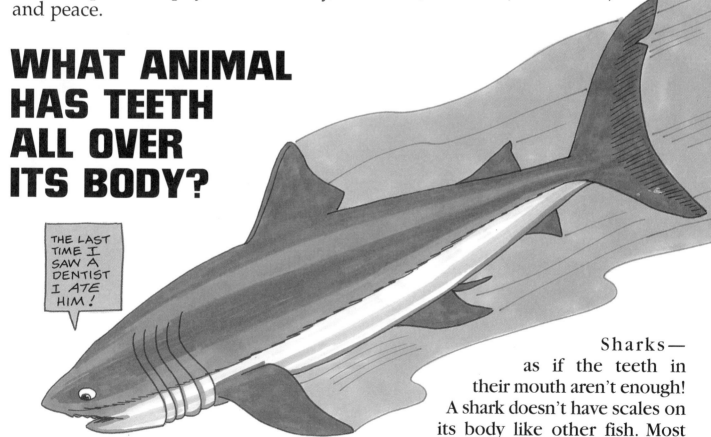

THE LAST TIME I SAW A DENTIST I ATE HIM!

Sharks— as if the teeth in their mouth aren't enough! A shark doesn't have scales on its body like other fish. Most sharks have *denticles* instead. A shark's body is covered with these small, razor-sharp, toothlike constructions. Denticles overlap like scales, but if you rubbed up against them, they would rip right through your skin!

# What happened during the GOLD RUSH?

During the 1800s in North America there were several gold discoveries. As soon as someone discovered gold, people "rushed" to the spot hoping to get rich. California, Colorado, and Alaska are the most famous gold-digging spots. In 1848, gold was found near a small town called San Francisco. A year later, 25,000 people lived there. In just one more year, there were so many miners in the territory that California had enough people to become a state.

# Where is the world's BIGGEST gingerbread house?

It was in Iowa, a state more famous for corn than gingerbread. In December of 1988, 100 people put together 2,000 sheets of gingerbread and 1,650 pounds of frosting. Their masterpiece was as tall as a five-story house—52 feet high—until everyone ate it!

# How does an egg hatch?

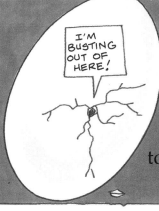

It's all in the tooth—the egg tooth. Both baby birds and reptiles chip their way out of a shell with a small, sharp tooth. A bird's egg tooth grows on its beak. A snake's is on its upper jaw. After the work of hatching is done, the egg tooth falls away.

## Who built the GIGANTIC statues on Easter Island and why?

It remains a mystery, but most experts believe it was the Polynesians who lived on Easter Island 2,000 years ago. Whoever built the statues used only stone tools. Most of the square-shaped human figures weigh about 20 tons, but the biggest weighs around 50 tons and stands 69 feet tall. Hundreds of the enormous statues, built on temple platforms, face the empty landscape. Scholars believe they are images of chiefs or spiritual leaders, but we may never know their true story.

## WHY IS IT HOTTER NEAR THE EQUATOR?

The equator is the great imaginary line that circles Earth halfway between the North and South Poles. It's this location that makes the equator such a hot spot. Because the Earth is curved, the most direct sunlight rays strike at the equator. The least direct sunlight hits the poles. But in Ecuador, a country on the equator, the city of Quito has a very high elevation. The altitude cools the temperature down to an average of about 58°F.

# What is the world's most popular spectator sport?

Soccer, which has been popular for quite a while. A ball made of animal skins may have been kicked around in ancient China. But other countries want to take credit for soccer, including Japan, Mexico, and Greece. Native Americans played a game in the 1600s called *pasuckuakohowog*, which means "they gather to play ball with the foot." The English finally set down regular rules for the game in 1863. Today, soccer is played in 140 nations and the whole world watches it!

## WHY DO FLEAS LIVE ON CATS AND DOGS?

Your pets are the fleas' dinner. Warm-blooded animals such as cats, dogs, squirrels, birds, and even humans are all on the flea menu. Blood is what fleas are after. Fleas can be controlled with certain kinds of chemicals called insecticides, as well as ordinary soap! Believe it or not, staying clean helps make your pet unfit for fleas to grow on. A flea collar coated with chemicals helps, too!

## What animal has eyes at the end of its arms, and feet under its arms?

The starfish. The "sea star" (its real name) is not necessarily a star and not a fish at all. It's a creature that lives in the ocean and takes several shapes. The most common is the five-pointed star—five "arms" with a body in the center.

The sea star "sees" with a small colored eyespot at the tip of each arm. These eyespots sense light but can't form images. The feet are rows of slender tubes that extend from the body to the end of each arm. With a suction disk at each tip, the sea star crawls along the ocean floor.

# WHERE WAS THE WORLD'S BIGGEST FIREWORKS DISPLAY?

It was not for the Fourth of July. The big bang was in Hokkaido, Japan in 1988 at the Lake Toya Festival. The flash and light started with a 1,543-pound shell that exploded, lighting the sky in a giant circle of fireworks that covered almost a mile!

# How is a bridge made?

Very carefully! The idea behind all bridges is to build a structure that shifts its weight to places where it can be supported. There are four main types of bridges.

**Beam bridge:** A flat road goes across a short, shallow river. It's held up by a long line of straight piers (supports) placed in the river floor.

**Arch bridge:** The road is placed over one or more arches built over the river. The weight of the road creates pressure that shifts down each side of the bridge to the "feet" anchored in the earth.

**Cantilever bridge:** There are two sections, one on each side of the river. The balance between the two sides supports a road between them.

WE ALL HAVE TOLLS!

**Suspension bridge:** The road is hung from giant, thick steel cables. These anchored cables shift the road's weight to the ground. One of the best-known suspension bridges is the Golden Gate Bridge in San Francisco, California.

# What is NASA?

The National Aeronautics and Space Administration. NASA is an organization in the United States that manages the development and operation of aircrafts in space. It all began in 1958 and has included everything from the first manned flight, to landing on the moon, to satellites that explore other planets, to space shuttles and space stations. Most NASA flights take off from the Kennedy Space Center in Cape Canaveral, Florida. NASA's "command center" is in Houston, Texas.

## Who were the Maya?

People who spoke the Mayan language and whose civilization reached its greatest height from A.D. 200 to 800. The Maya lived in what is now areas of Belize, Guatemala, El Salvador, and Mexico. Many years before the Europeans, the Maya developed a calendar and used mathematics. They also created an advanced form of writing. Their pottery and sculpture is treasured today, and some of their magnificent temples are still standing. Four million Maya still speak the old languages and keep the ancient traditions alive.

## WHAT IS SOLAR HEATING?

Sun power, which creates a great deal of heat. But it's difficult to capture the heat, store it, and use it when you need it. Solar heating is an effort to do just that. Special plates installed on the roof of a house absorb heat from the sun. Once absorbed, the heat is stored in water or rocks in a large container. A heating system circulates the heat throughout the house. Even experimental solar-powered cars have been built!

## HOW BIG WAS THE WORLD'S BIGGEST SNOWMAN?

If you were on the top floor of a six-story building and stuck your head out the window, you could be nose to nose with the world's biggest snowman. In Alaska, in 1988, a group of people who probably like cold weather spent two weeks building "Super Frosty." When they were done, Frosty the Snowman had a 62-foot-high big brother!

# WHY DOES THE MOON LOOK LIKE SWISS CHEESE?

Swiss cheese has holes. The moon has craters, or pits, in the surface. Some of the craters are small, but others are huge—up to 155 miles across—and can be seen from Earth. Most of the craters were made during early periods of the solar system, when space was a traffic jam of rocks and metal flying off the planets as they formed. When these fragments crashed into the moon, the impact caused craters.

## Why do babies cry?

To communicate. Babies can't say "I'm so hungry I could eat a horse" or "Get me out of this car seat." So they make the only noise they can—crying. If you're around a baby, you can tell the difference between crying that means hungry, angry, tired, or scared.

## Where does the word "Eureka" come from?

Greece. Archimedes (287-212 B.C.) was a Greek mathematician and inventor. The story is that he had just stepped into one of the public baths when an idea came to him. He was so excited that he rushed home yelling "Eureka! Eureka!" (I have found it! I have found it!) So when you discover something you've been looking for, shout "Eureka!"

## WHAT IS A MARSUPIAL?

Kangaroos are the most famous marsupials, but some others are opossums, koalas, and wombats. What makes them different from other animals is the "pouch" just below their stomach. The pouch is for carrying their offspring.

Marsupial babies do more of their growing outside the mother's body than inside. At birth, they are very underdeveloped and less than an inch long. These tiny creatures struggle up through their mother's fur and crawl into her pouch. Inside they find nipples for milk and a safe place to hide. A baby kangaroo stays there for five to ten months.

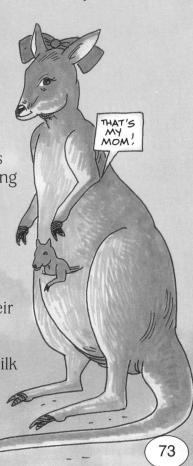

THAT'S MY MOM!

73

# Who was Gandhi?

Mohandas Gandhi (1869-1948) guided India to independence from Britain. Called the *Mahatma*, meaning "great soul," Gandhi believed in nonviolence, courage, and truth. At times, he fasted to show belief in his cause. In 1948, one year after India was granted independence, conflicts broke out between Muslims and Hindus. Gandhi encouraged them to live peacefully, and was killed by a Hindu who disagreed with him.

I'M HUNGRY!

## HOW DOES A CLAM EAT?

It opens its shell slightly to let dinner in. Tiny hairs filter food into a small mouth, then into the stomach. The food is digested there and absorbed into the intestines. Clams eat tiny water plants and sea animals called plankton. Although clams seem to be bloblike creatures, they have a digestive system, and even a heart and blood vessels.

# HOW DOES MY VOICE WORK?

It's all in your vocal cords, a pair of muscles in your windpipe. When air from your lungs passes over your vocal cords, they vibrate. To make sounds, your vocal cords need to contract, or tighten, rather than relax. You control that. The more your vocal cords contract, the more high-pitched the sound.

Your mouth and tongue form these sounds into words.

# Why does the word "LOVE" mean ZERO POINTS in tennis?

It certainly doesn't mean tennis players love to lose! The answer is hidden between two languages. Tennis began in France in the 1100s or 1200s. "Love" may have come from the French word *l'oeuf*, which was slang for zero. The English, who invented the modern version of tennis in the late 1800s, pronounced it "luff." Eventually, it became love.

# WHO INVENTED PLAYING CARDS?

MY MUMMY TAUGHT ME HOW TO PLAY CARDS.

History has hidden the answer. People must have been too busy playing to stop and say, "Hey, who made up this game?" Most scholars believe that some form of cards began in India and developed in Egypt in the 12th and 13th centuries. By 1380, cards were known in Italy, Switzerland, France, and Spain. In 1452, playing cards were burned in bonfires as a reaction to gambling.

# What is the Venus flytrap?

The Venus flytrap is one of 500 types of *carnivorous*, or meat-eating, plants. The plant eats mostly insects though, so don't worry. The two-sided leaves of the Venus are the "fly trap." Each is lined with toothlike spines. When an insect flies inside and touches the trigger hairs...SNAP! The two sides of the leaf clamp together. The insect is caught and slowly digested (it takes about 10 days). Finally, the leaf opens again. After two or three catches, the leaves die and are replaced by younger, snappier leaves.

LUNCH TIME!

# WHAT IS A WINDMILL USED FOR?

Windmills use the force of the wind to produce power. Wind whips through the blades, which are attached to a shaft. The shaft, which runs down the tower, is connected to an underground pump or mechanical gears. Windmills are used for such tasks as milling grain, pumping water for farmland, pressing oil from seeds, and grinding different materials. Wind turbine generators use the power of the wind to generate electricity. They have huge, propellerlike blades.

# What was the PONY EXPRESS?

Eighty mailmen on horseback. The pony express was a well organized mail-delivery system that operated between Missouri and California. In the 1860s, it took teamwork to get mail to its destination. Riders galloped at full speed, stopping at stations every ten miles or so to change horses. Each rider traveled up to 100 miles of the total route—1,966 miles. They hauled the mail in pouches, carrying two guns and a knife to protect themselves against bandits. The whole trip was made in about eight or nine days. One of the riders was 14-year-old William Cody, later known as Buffalo Bill.

# How are fossils formed? Where are they found?

When an animal or plant dies, it decays over time. Sometimes, if conditions are right, the earth preserves traces of the animal or plant—for millions of years! Imagine an ancient reptile that died in mud. Its flesh would decay. The bones would slowly dissolve, but minerals might fill in the spaces, harden, and preserve the shape of the bones. That's called a *petrified* fossil. A *mold* fossil is created when an animal or plant dies and its shape forms an impression in the earth. Fossils are found all over the world in places where ancient rocks have been uncovered.

I WAS IN AN ACCIDENT.

## DO INSECTS HAVE A HEART AND BLOOD?

Yes—tiny as they may be, insects have pretty complicated working parts. Their heart is a long tube that runs along the top of the body. It pumps blood, which brings digested food to the organs and takes away waste materials. But the blood doesn't carry oxygen, so it isn't red like ours. It's (yuck!) green or blue.

THAT'S MY PET CAT,

# Why is a black cat considered unlucky?

If you fear a black cat crossing your path, blame it on witches. Witchcraft has been around since ancient times. At one time, people believed that each witch had an assistant, or personal demon, called a familiar. Familiars took the form of animals— and many were black cats.

I AM?!

## Why does Saturn have rings around it?

NOT THAT KIND OF RING!

The planet is surrounded by chunks of ice, plus some dust and metal materials. These particles orbit around Saturn like satellites. Also orbiting Saturn are small *moonlets*, celestial bodies with their own gravitational pull. Scientists believe that the pull of these moonlets keeps the particles together, forming the rings. The rings whirl around Saturn, shining with light coming from the sun.

## How are animals trained?

YUM! I DID GOOD!

Most animals learn by a method called *operant conditioning*. Basically, each time an animal performs a behavior the trainer has in mind, it receives a reward. The reward is called a *reinforcer* because it reinforces, or encourages, the behavior. Animals don't "think" as we do, but they can learn behaviors in this way. Gorillas, chimpanzees, and marine mammals are trained by this method.

## Who was SACAJAWEA?

FOLLOW ME.

A Native American woman, of the Shoshone tribe, who made an important contribution to the exploration of America. In 1804, explorers Meriwether Lewis and William Clark set out from St. Louis to find a route to the west coast. Sacajawea went with them as a guide. Their journey would have been much harder without her. She saved them weeks of travel time because she knew the territory and the mountain passes. She found food when it was scarce by gathering wild plants. Lewis and Clark were so grateful, they named a river, a mountain peak, and a mountain pass in her honor.

# Does a rain dance work?

If it did, we would have rain whenever our rivers run dry or when crops need water. Many ancient cultures believed that the important forces of nature, like the sun, the earth, and the rain, were gods. It was their way of explaining how the universe worked. To them, it made sense to pray to the god of rain if rain were needed. Many of the songs and dances in these rituals were very beautiful.

## WHEN WERE FORKS INVENTED?

The first forks probably had two prongs and were used to hold meat over a fire. It wasn't until the 1500s in Italy that forks were used at the table, and then only by people who cared enough to keep their shirtsleeves out of their food. Still, forks weren't very common. If you think about it, most foods can be eaten without a fork—but it's hard to eat soup without a spoon!

# WHAT'S THE OLDEST INSECT?

The cockroach! Those pesky pests have been around for 350 million years, and they look pretty much the same now as they did then. They have flat bodies, long legs, and range from about one-quarter inch to three inches long. What incredible survivors!

*I'VE BEEN AROUND!*

# How FAST can a cheetah run?

Seventy miles an hour in 25-foot leaps. When it comes to short distances, the cheetah is the fastest land animal on earth. The cat's flexible spine is the secret to its speed. The spine curls and uncurls like elastic, springing the cheetah forward. Speedier than a sports car, the cat bursts from zero to 40 miles per hour in two seconds!

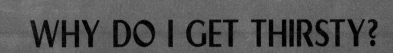

*I GOT A TICKET FOR SPEEDING!*

*SPEEDING TICKET - 40 MPH IN A 20 MPH ZONE*

# WHY DO I GET THIRSTY?

*ANCHOVY PIZZA MAKES ME THIRSTY!!*

Your body is trying to tell you something. It's saying you don't have enough water in your bloodstream. Strangely, people who are dehydrated (seriously lacking water) tend to drink just what they need. Scientists think we must have a "water meter" in our bodies, but they haven't found it yet. Salty food also makes us thirsty because salt absorbs water. When you drink enough water to satisfy your body, your thirst is quenched!

IT'S A WHALE OF A PLACE!

NORTH POLE

# WHAT'S THE DIFFERENCE BETWEEN THE ARCTIC AND THE ANTARCTIC?

The Arctic is home of the North Pole. The Arctic Circle, an imaginary line 1,630 miles below the Pole, marks the entire region—including the Arctic Ocean, many islands, and northern parts of Europe, Asia, and North America. It's very cold in the Arctic, but in some areas the snow disappears in the summer. The Arctic is home to polar bears, seals, whales, musk oxen, caribou, and birds.

The Antarctic is home of the South Pole. The region covers over five million square miles. At its greatest distance, the icy continent of Antarctica is 3,250 miles across. A few mosses and just two flowering plants manage to survive—along with a small, wingless fly. The Antarctic Ocean is home to fish, birds, seals, whales, and penguins.

SOUTH POLE

IT'S A WHALE OF A PLACE!

# Where did the expression "GOING BANANAS" come from?

We say someone is "going bananas" when they're being silly or ridiculous. Monkeys can act pretty crazy, swinging from trees, whooping and calling—and they do love bananas. So, "going bananas" is the human version of all this monkey business.

I NEED A SHAVE!

# What is a werewolf?

A mythical person who changes into a wolf and back into a human again—if you believe it. Werewolves appear in many myths and stories. They are not the type of animal you'd want for a pet. Generally, they bite people and they aren't too cute. Evil or magic power is said to lurk around them. In some cultures, legends claim that people turn into tigers, foxes, leopards, or jaguars. In "were-world," this is known as shape shifting.

| Buddhism | Christianity | Hinduism | Islam | Judaism | Taoism |
|----------|--------------|----------|-------|---------|--------|

## How many religions are there in the world?

The religions that are most organized, and that have the most followers today, are Buddhism, Christianity, Hinduism, Islam, Judaism, and Taoism. That makes six, but there are many other religions practiced around the world.

# What is the Parthenon?

A surviving building of the ancient world. The Parthenon is a temple in Athens, Greece, built in the fifth century B.C. to honor Athena, goddess of war, peace, and wisdom. It stands on a hill called the Acropolis, which overlooks the city. Many of the sculptures from the Parthenon are considered among the world's greatest works of art.

# Who invented the YO-YO?

Yo-yos were known in ancient China and Greece, but the Philippines put the yo-yo on the modern map. In the 16th century, Filipinos used yo-yos to snare animal prey from trees. As you can imagine, Filipinos became very good yo-yo players! In 1920, American Donald F. Duncan saw a Filipino man yo-yoing. Soon after, Duncan went into the yo-yo business and made it the world's most famous toy. Since then, going "Around the World" has become a well-known maneuver. In 1992, a yo-yo went aboard the space shuttle Atlantis and traveled 3,321,007 miles—going around the world, for real, 127 times!

# What is Dr. Seuss's REAL NAME?

Theodor Seuss Geisel (1904–1991)—better known as Dr. Seuss, the Pulitzer prize-winning author of 47 children's books. His work takes place in a silly make-believe world filled with truffula trees, ziffs and zuffs, and nerkles and nerds, but each book has something to say to adults and children about real life. "I like nonsense," Dr. Seuss has said. "It wakes up the brain cells." Among his most famous books are *The Cat in the Hat, Green Eggs and Ham,* and *How the Grinch Stole Christmas.*

## WHY DO WE BREATHE?

We breathe because every cell in the body needs oxygen from the air to stay alive. When air comes into the lungs, oxygen is passed into the bloodstream. The bloodstream carries oxygen to the cells. Along the way, blood picks up waste called carbon dioxide and returns it to the lungs, where it is breathed out. Breathing is automatic—we don't have to think about it. You take about 20,000 breaths a day, which could add up to over 600 million in your lifetime.

# How is RUBBER made?

I'M A BIG SAP!

Natural rubber comes from the sap of certain trees, and synthetic rubber is made by people. Rubber trees are found mostly in tropical climates. To make the trees' sap into a useful product called *latex*, water is removed and chemicals are added. The latex is then rolled into rubber sheets. Synthetic rubber is made from coal, oil, and natural gas. Rubber is one of the most useful products in the world. It holds air and keeps out moisture. It's elastic and durable. Some of the rubber products we use are tires, boots, raincoats, balls, erasers, and, of course, rubber bands!

# Who was the youngest ruler of a nation?

A two-year-old boy, Emperor Hsuan T'ung, the last emperor of China. He was born in 1906. Just six years later, a revolution swept the country and everything changed. Henry P'u-i, as the young emperor was known, was forced to leave China. He did return, but was put in jail. Finally, for the 10 years before he died in 1967, T'ung was allowed to work as a gardener at one of the colleges in Beijing, the capital of China. So, at the end of his life, the last emperor was ruled by others.

## WHAT IS THE FASTEST TRAIN?

The TGV (Train à Grande Vitesse), a high-speed electric train system in France. There are more than 350 trains that run on the TGV. The fastest one, so far, is the Atlantique. Its average cruising speed is 186 miles per hour. The company is planning an even speedier version. The TGV 2000 is expected to cruise at 217 miles per hour.

I'M ALMOST FASTER THAN A SPEEDING BULLET!

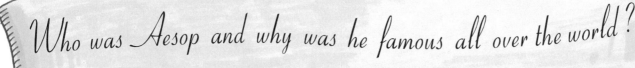

## Who was Aesop and why was he famous all over the world?

DO YOU WANT TO RACE?

Aesop was a Greek storyteller who lived from about 620 to 560 B.C. Since then, his fables have circled the world. Fables tell us about human behavior. In *The Tortoise and the Hare*, the two animals run a race. The speedy rabbit is so sure of winning that he takes his time and even naps. But the slow tortoise "keeps on trucking" and wins the race. Aesop's moral, or lesson, is that determination and steady work will get you where you want to go every time.

SURE! HO-HUM.

READY? SET? GO!!

# HOW DO TERMITES BUILD A MOUND?

Termites build big homes called "mounds" by cementing bits of soil together with their saliva. There are many different types of termites, but the big builders live in colonies that can have millions of members. Their mounds can be 20 to 30 feet high, filled with a maze of tunnels and chambers. Each colony has workers, soldiers, and a king and queen who live in a central chamber. The queen is enormous compared to the others. Her job is to lay thousands of eggs a day. Such termites are most common in warm regions in Africa, Australia, and South America.

*IT'S A LOT OF WORK!*

# What is LEVITATION?

*WOW!*

Have you ever seen a magician float a person in the air? That's levitation. How is it done? It's the magician's secret, but you can be sure it's a trick. Some people, however, believe we can use mind power to make people or objects levitate. The closest most people come to levitating is floating in a swimming pool!

*HOW TO DO MAGIC*

*IT WORKS!*

# WHAT IS THE WORLD'S SMALLEST COUNTRY?

It's a country within a city within a country. Vatican City in Rome, Italy, is an independent country governed by the Roman Catholic Church. The Pope lives there. Its total area is only one fifth of a square mile, a distance you could easily walk.

*ITALY*

*VATICAN CITY*

*ZIP!*

They really don't. Starlight passes through our atmosphere, and that's where the "twinkling" begins. Dust, smoke, and other particles are always dancing about in the atmosphere. All those swirling particles interfere with a star's light. The star appears to dim and brighten. Also, the atmosphere bends, or *refracts*, the light rays. These influences create the special effect we call twinkling.

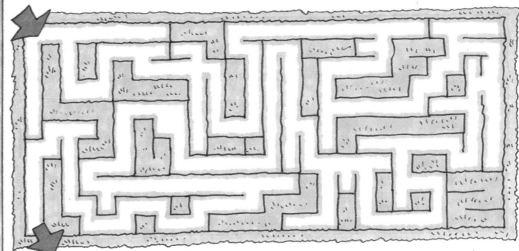

# WHAT IS THE WORLD'S LARGEST MAZE?

The world's largest maze was made in a cornfield in Shippensburg, Pennsylvania, in 1995. It covered 172,225 square feet and its zigzag path was 2.03 miles long. But it didn't last. It took only about two months for the grass to grow back.

## Where does petroleum oil come from?

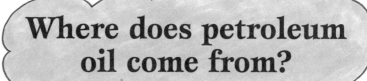

Underground. Scientists believe that ancient plants and marine organisms are the source of petroleum. As the sea life decomposed, it became trapped in rocks or covered with mud at the bottom of the sea. Over millions of years, carbon and other substances left behind formed oil. Much of the world's petroleum has been found in the Middle East. Petroleum oil is still being formed, but not as fast as the world uses it up.

OIL!

# Who made the Statue of Liberty?

Frederic Bartholdi designed the statue and Alexandre Eiffel (who designed the Eiffel Tower) built the framework. The grand lady with the torch was given to the United States by France as a symbol of friendship. It represents the liberty of living under a free form of government. Constructed and shipped to the United States in parts, the statue was erected on Liberty Island in New York Harbor in 1886. *Liberty Enlightening the World* (her full name) is one of the largest statues in the world. It's more than 151 feet, from the sandals to the top of the torch, and weighs 450,000 pounds.

# HOW DOES A FIGURE SKATER SPIN AROUND *SO FAST?*

Changing one type of posture to another increases the "rotation rate," or speed of a spin. Say a skater is spinning with her arms outstretched—then she pulls her arms in close to her body. She's going to spin faster because the *momentum,* or energy, from her limbs is passed on to her body.

I CAN'T SKATE!

I'M DIZZY WATCHING!

## HOW HOT IS LIGHTNING?

Lightning is electricity leaping between a positive and negative charge—and it's hot. Air within a lightning stroke may reach 54,000°F. The intense heat causes the air to expand and then contract as it cools. This wildly vibrating air ripples away from the lightning as sound waves. We hear the vibrations as thunder.

## Who was the first person to sign the Declaration of Independence?

John Hancock (1737-1793), president of the Continental Congress, the first governing body of the American colonies. His signature was so important-looking that it inspired a saying. When someone signs a document, that person is said to be signing his or her "John Hancock."

NO! MY HAND IS NOT COLD!

## WHO WAS NAPOLEON?

Napoleon Bonaparte (1769-1821) created an empire that covered most of western and central Europe. Proclaimed emperor of France in 1804 and king of Italy in 1805, Napoleon was a military genius who also contributed important ideas about government, education, and banking. However, Napoleon's downfall came with the Battle of Waterloo in 1815, which ended French domination of Europe. He was defeated and exiled to an island off Africa called St. Helena, where he died.

# INDEX